THE ART OF WAR

LANDMARK EDITION

THE ART OF WAR

LANDMARK EDITION

The classic of strategy annotated
and introduced by Mitch Horowitz

SUN TZU

TRANSLATED BY LIONEL GILES
INCLUDES THE TRANSLATOR'S EDITION OF THE *TAO TE CHING*

MEDIA

Published 2021 by Gildan Media LLC
aka G&D Media
www.GandDmedia.com

Front Cover design by David Rheinhardt of Pyrographx

Interior design by Meghan Day Healey of Story Horse, LLC

Library of Congress Cataloging-in-Publication Data is available upon
request

ISBN: 978-1-7225-0560-8

10   9   8   7   6   5   4   3   2   1

Contents

Individual tables on content appear at the start of each section

Introduction
Nature and Conflict

By Mitch Horowitz

"The violent and stiff-necked die not by a natural death."
—LAO TZU, *Tao Te Ching*, translated by Lionel Giles

The Art of War is essentially a Taoist work. Its core principle is to blend with the natural order of things. That is the book's approach to conflict and friction as it is to restoration and maintenance of peace. I believe that the book's outlook can be distilled to five basic points:

1. The greatest warrior prevails without fighting; rightness (or the Tao), preparation, and advantage make conflict unnecessary.

2. Beware the devastation of conflict; war should never be pursued lightly.

3. Be eminently watchful: know your enemy, know yourself, know your terrain. Fight only if victory is assured.

4. When you strike, concentrate fury and power at your enemy's weakest point.

5. When conflict ends, quickly restore peace. Protracted conflict destroys victor and vanquished alike.

Although *The Art of War* is written from a martial perspective, its five ideals are Taoism itself. They counsel the reader to function like nature—the author's definition of "rightness": Life tends towards generativity and reproduction in all its expressions; but in order for nature to perpetuate itself there exist innate ruptures, such as a forest fire clearing away old brush; if left untouched, the brush would eventually overrun and choke the forest. Nature is not spiteful or protractive. It works by direct and unimpeded means. The forest fire first takes dead leaves, branches, and underbrush. It eventually abates. And life returns. As an oceanographer once put it to me: "Life is what planets do"—the ecosystem of a planet or solar system (gravity itself abets life) creates homeostasis. Seen in a certain light, that is an expression of the Tao, or Way.

There is no simple manner of identifying the author of *The Art of War.* Nor is it entirely clear that there existed a single author. The book is traditionally attributed to

Zhou dynasty general Sun Tzu (c. 544 BC–496 BC), an honorific title meaning "Master Sun."

The legendary warrior is said to have recorded his insights around 500 BC, although some historians argue for a later date. Beyond parables, very little is known about this warrior who does not formally appear in ancient Chinese historical literature until soon after 100 BC, four centuries following his recorded death. In this sense, Sun Tzu is somewhat like the Hellenic sage Pythagoras (c. 570 BC–495 BC), with whom, if certain records are accepted, he shares contemporaneous ancestry, and whose life, like Master Sun's, is known to us from writings that followed the philosopher's death sometimes by centuries.

It is likewise important to understand that other primeval writers and sages, including Homer and Socrates, did not possess clearly demarcated historical identities, although consensus holds that such figures may have existed either as single personas or composites. During the Renaissance, for example, scholars and translators marveled at the Greek-Egyptian writings attributed to Hermes Trismegistus, or thrice-greatest Hermes, a Greek title for Egypt's god of intellect, Thoth. Hermes Trismegistus was considered a psychopomp of great antiquity. Later scholarship demonstrated that the writings attributed to Hermes, or the Hermetica, actually dated to late antiquity, probably in the decades immediately following the death of Christ. The author's name was attached to these works by multiple scribes who, in a practice not uncommon in antiquity, affixed the byline of a mythical or venerated figure to their writings in order to lend them greater gravity or authority. That is not a mark of inauthenticity. The Hermetic literature is likely a retention of very ancient oral tradition written down in expository form in the closing centuries of Ancient Egyptian civilization. In that sense, the Hermetica is a vital expression of humanity's primeval insight regardless of authorship.[*]

In the modern West, we are accustomed to view writing as the work of distinct authors with personal insights. But, as alluded, that model did not necessarily prevail among early-ancient philosophers and historians. In both the East and West, the more common practice was for scribes—versus authors with fixed personas—to reproduce the outlook of philosophical schools, military orders, governments, and religious castes. That is the process by which Scripture itself was written. Hence, in terms of the history of ideas, it matters less "who" wrote *The Art of War*—if there was a single author—than the historical integrity of its verses. In that vein, the Taoist

---

[*] On this theme, see my article "The New Age and Gnosticism: Terms of Commonality," *Gnosis: Journal of Gnostic Studies*, 13 Nov 2019, Volume 4: Issue 2. I explore the same thesis in a more popular form in *The Kybalion Study Guide* (2020, G&D Media).

naturalism and deep antiquity of *The Art of War* make the short work perhaps the most enduring and widely read expression of Ancient Chinese philosophy—or possibly of any branch of philosophy—of our era.

Given the book's vast number of modern reproductions and its ubiquitous appeal, *The Art of War* may, in our generation, be even more widely read than the similarly mysterious and almost certainly older work on whose insights it rests: the *Tao Te Ching*, attributed to the mythical 6th century BC sage Lao Tzu, meaning "Old Master." If search-engine results are any guide, *The Art of War* has significantly more eyes on it than its ancestral work.

It is not difficult to understand why the younger book may have surpassed the older in readership. Although the *Tao Te Ching* soars on philosophical wings, *The Art of War*, at times similarly lyrical, gets straight down to business: its aim is not, or not solely, numinous and naturalistic insight but hardcore victory.

Of the two legendary sages, Lao Tzu and Sun Tzu, the general Master Sun has a greater hold on the popular mind. Sun Tzu's insights are eagerly absorbed today by managers, athletes, financiers, self-help practitioners, and general go-getters. And to that constituency, Master Sun delivers: he addresses conflict and victory as matters of brutal efficiency. But it behooves would-be warriors to note the closing lines of the *Tao Te Ching*, which express an outlook at the foundation of the general's own point of view: "He who proceeds violently across the earth will die a weary death. Know this, and you know all my teachings."

The Art of War as we experience it in translation is a modern work. Its public history in the West can be roughly traced to 1772 when a Jesuit missionary to Peking, Father Jean Joseph Marie Amiot (1718–1793), published a French translation in Paris. The book was feted in the press and speculation held that it was read by Napoleon himself. It was not until 1905, however, that the work got translated into English by Captain Everard Ferguson Calthrop (1876–1915), a British naval officer stationed in Tokyo. History has not been kind to his effort. British Sinologist and translator of the present volume, Lionel Giles (1875–1958), wrote in his original introduction: "Unfortunately, it was evident that the translator's knowledge of Chinese was far too scanty to fit him to grapple with the manifold difficulties of Sun Tzu. He himself plainly acknowledges that without the aid of two Japanese gentlemen 'the accompanying translation would have been impossible.' We can only wonder, then, that with their help it should have been so excessively bad."

Giles proved as enterprising as he was blunt. An assistant curator at the British Museum and caretaker of the Department of Oriental Manuscripts and Printed

Books, as well as the son of an influential British diplomat and Chinese linguist, Herbert Giles, the scholar in 1910 produced his own painstaking, elegant, and enticingly spare translation of *The Art of War*. Giles' sculpted and meticulous prose set the standard for nearly every translation that followed, of which there were dozens. It forms the basis for this volume. Although new translations arrive steadily today—and there is always room for points of clarity and refinement, both textual and historical—none, in my reading, have surpassed the clarity and precision of Giles' effort.

This raises the question of whether what appears in this volume is, in fact, Giles' original work. To that, the answer is yes and no. The prose is strictly his. The number scheme of this translation, in which each verse is ordered consecutively by chapter, follows Giles' original. But it should be noted straight out that Giles' 1910 publication was accompanied by the ancient Chinese characters as well as the translator's extensive footnotes, in which he expanded on language or textual points and sometimes added historical commentary. These notes and characters do not appear in this volume. Is there an injustice or incompleteness in providing Giles' verses without their original commentary?

There is, in fact, precedent for such publication— approved by the translator himself. In 1944, Giles granted permission to The Military Service Publishing Company of Harrisburg, Pennsylvania, to issue his stripped-down translation for military and general readers. His and the publisher's hugely serviceable act preserved, popularized, and familiarized the reading public with this vital work. In his introduction to the 1944 edition, Brigadier General Thomas R. Phillips of the U.S. Army wrote: "The critical notes of the translator, which comprise the larger portion of his book, have been summarized in the text whenever they had military value. Other translations in English and French lack both the accuracy and crystalline language which distinguish Dr. Giles. Grateful acknowledgment is made to Dr. Giles and Luzac & Co. [Giles' London-based publisher] for their generous permission to use his translation."

That precedent-setting edition also omitted Giles' original number scheme (restored here) and flowed his text together under new subheadings. The bracketed annotations within the 1944 edition were heavily geared toward immediate concerns of winning World War II, as were the subheads, which included titles like "Blitzkrieg." This edition opts for a more universal reproduction of Giles' 1910 translation, which I believe excels on its own. I have supplemented the work with footnotes that highlight key meanings, resolve potential disclarity, and provide historical context. Otherwise, the ascetic brilliance of Giles' verses appear on their own.

But this volume does more than provide a serviceable rendering of the 1910 translation. This Landmark Edition is, to my knowledge, the first reproduction of Giles' original that includes his seminally important 1905 translation of the *Tao Te Ching,* or, as he titled it, *The Sayings of Lao Tzu*. And this returns me to a point made at the beginning of this introduction. *The Art of War* stands on the shoulders of the *Tao Te Ching*. To read the two in concert is to experience a fuller understanding of the Taoist wisdom of both works.* As alluded earlier, the Tao, meaning roughly Way, signifies the natural flow of the universe. It is the underlying order of creation and the eternal flow of harmony behind and through all beings and events. Functioning within the Tao means functioning as a natural being—and, in the vision of Sun Tzu, a victorious warrior.

Why should any of this background matter? Is an ancient martial work and its Taoist antecedent really useful to contemporary readers? I contend that these works are useful, and perhaps urgent, on two counts: practical and ethical, although the two concerns are not really different, another Taoist principle.

As Sun Tzu taught, there are periods when friction or conflict appear on your path. In the Taoist view, this

---

* To facilitate this cross-reading, this volume includes an integrated index of *The Art of War* and the *Tao Te Ching*. I also make comparative comments in the footnotes.

experience is not a rupture with nature but an expression of it. When contention occurs, we face five basic choices, as we do in all general situations. These five choices can be extrapolated from the still-older Chinese oracular work the *I-Ching* (c. late 9th century BC): 1) stop, 2) go back cautiously, 3) go back rapidly, 4) move ahead cautiously, or 5) move ahead energetically. Seen in light of Taoist philosophy, none of these courses is "better" or more honorable than the other. The question is: which is in alignment with the Tao?

In helping you make that determination, *The Art of War* is a wonder of practical wisdom. But the work has broader ethical and social implications. British military historian Captain B. H. Liddell Hart (1895–1970), one of the clearest and canniest voices of military historicism of the twentieth century, observed in 1963: "Civilization might have been spared much of the damage suffered in the world wars of this century if the influence of [Carl von] Clausewitz's monumental tomes *On War*, which moulded European military thought in the era preceding the First World War, had been blended with and balanced by a knowledge of Sun Tzu's exposition on 'The Art of War'." The martial philosophy of the Prussian general and military strategist Clausewitz normalized war as an extension of state policy—"politics by other means," he called it. Clausewitz further taught that once war is undertaken it must be pursued to its absolute ends. The sole requisite of conflict, Clausewitz wrote, is using any and every means to decimate the enemy.

For some post-war Western commanders, especially in the wake of America's defeat in Vietnam, Clausewitz's work represented a back-to-basics realism and a repudiation of idealistic notions of waging "limited war." But to Liddle Hart, the Prussian's endorsement of totalized warfare, and his tone of cold logic in pursuing destruction, contrasted poorly with Sun Tzu's "realism and moderation." For Sun Tzu, war was not a neutral extension of politics but a grave and final resort whose risks must be mitigated; and, while victory was essential to Sun Tzu's doctrine, he saw the ultimate aim of war as restoration of normalcy.

In terms that would have sounded offkey if not alien to Clausewitz and his disciples, Sun Tzu stressed the need to think flexibly about objectives. For example, Sun Tzu cautioned in chapter VII: "Do not interfere with an army that is returning home. When you surround an army, leave an outlet free. Do not press a desperate foe too hard." The teacher counselled that if you press a desperate person too hard you ensure that he will fight to the death (not a bad metaphorical principle in managing family and workplace conflicts), which will increase casualties on both sides. Hence, in Sun Tzu's teaching, the canny general permits a retreating foe to disengage.

* * *

My hope is that your reading of *The Art of War* alongside Giles' translation of the *Tao Te Ching* will provide you—at times joltingly—with a powerful new estimate and measure of personal behavior. In his 1938 *Guide to Kulchur*, the profoundly flawed but inescapably brilliant poet Ezra Pound (1885–1972) observed: "Properly, we shd. read for power. Man reading shd. be man intensely alive. The book shd. be a ball of light in one's hand." *The Art of War* is such a book of ethical power—not force, which dies with its user, but power which is generative and renewable. May this work suitably glow in your hands.

Mitch Horowitz is the PEN Award-winning author of books including Occult America, One Simple Idea, *and* The Miracle Club. *A writer-in-residence at the New York Public Library, his G&D Media titles include* The Miracle Habits *and* The Seeker's Guide to the Secret Teachings of All Ages. *Follow him on Twitter @MitchHorowitz and Instagram @MitchHorowitz23.*

Contents

I.

Laying Plans

1. Sun Tzu said: The art of war is of vital importance to the State.

2. It is a matter of life and death, a road either to safety or to ruin. Hence it is a subject of inquiry which can on no account be neglected.

3. The art of war, then, is governed by five constant factors, to be taken into account in one's deliberations, when seeking to determine the conditions obtaining in the field.

4. These are:
   (1) The Moral Law;[1]
   (2) Heaven;
   (3) Earth;
   (4) The Commander;
   (5) Method and discipline.

---

[1] This is sometimes translated as the Tao, or the Way, as explored in the introduction.

5,6. *The Moral Law* causes the people to be in complete accord with their ruler, so that they will follow him regardless of their lives, undismayed by any danger.

7. *Heaven* signifies night and day, cold and heat, times and seasons.

8. *Earth* comprises distances, great and small; danger and security; open ground and narrow passes; the chances of life and death.

9. *The Commander* stands for the virtues of wisdom, sincerity, benevolence, courage and strictness.

10. By *Method and discipline* are to be understood the marshaling of the army in its proper subdivisions, the graduations of rank among the officers, the maintenance of roads by which supplies may reach the army, and the control of military expenditure.

11. These five heads should be familiar to every general: he who knows them will be victorious; he who knows them not will fail.

12. Therefore, in your deliberations, when seeking to determine the military conditions, let them be made the basis of a comparison, in this wise:

13. (1) Which of the two sovereigns is imbued with the Moral law?

    (2) Which of the two generals has most ability?

    (3) With whom lie the advantages derived from Heaven and Earth?

    (4) On which side is discipline most rigorously enforced?

    (5) Which army is stronger?

    (6) On which side are officers and men more highly trained?

    (7) In which army is there the greater constancy both in reward and punishment?

14. By means of these seven considerations I can forecast victory or defeat.

15. The general that hearkens to my counsel and acts upon it, will conquer: let such a one be retained in command! The general that hearkens not to my counsel nor acts upon it, will suffer defeat: let such a one be dismissed!

16. While heading the profit of my counsel, avail yourself also of any helpful circumstances over and beyond the ordinary rules.

17. According as circumstances are favorable, one should modify one's plans.

18. All warfare is based on deception.[2]

19. Hence, when able to attack, we must seem unable; when using our forces, we must seem inactive; when we are near, we must make the enemy believe we are far away; when far away, we must make him believe we are near.

20. Hold out baits to entice the enemy. Feign disorder, and crush him.

21. If he is secure at all points, be prepared for him. If he is in superior strength, evade him.

22. If your opponent is of choleric temper, seek to irritate him. Pretend to be weak, that he may grow arrogant.

23. If he is taking his ease, give him no rest. If his forces are united, separate them.

---

[2] This is Sun Tzu's key strategic point; most tactics in the book stem from this principle.

24. Attack him where he is unprepared, appear where you are not expected.

25. These military devices, leading to victory, must not be divulged beforehand.

26. Now the general who wins a battle makes many calculations in his temple ere the battle is fought. The general who loses a battle makes but few calculations beforehand. Thus do many calculations lead to victory, and few calculations to defeat: how much more no calculation at all! It is by attention to this point that I can foresee who is likely to win or lose.[3]

---

[3] Sun Tzu had no respect for the commander who acted out of emotion or haste. Research, foreknowledge, deliberateness, and information-gathering are central to his system of warfare and are , he argued, the best guarantors of victory. See chapter IV of the *Tao Te Ching*: "The best soldiers are not warlike; the best fighters do not lose their temper."

II.

Waging War

1. Sun Tzu said: In the operations of war, where there are in the field a thousand swift chariots, as many heavy chariots, and a hundred thousand mail-clad soldiers, with provisions enough to carry them a thousand *li*,[4] the expenditure at home and at the front, including entertainment of guests, small items such as glue and paint, and sums spent on chariots and armor, will reach the total of a thousand ounces of silver per day. Such is the cost of raising an army of 100,000 men.

2. When you engage in actual fighting, if victory is long in coming, then men's weapons will grow dull and their ardor will be damped. If you lay siege to a town, you will exhaust your strength.

---

[4] A traditional Chinese unit of measure, a "*li*" is about 500 meters.

3. Again, if the campaign is protracted, the resources of the State will not be equal to the strain.[5]

4. Now, when your weapons are dulled, your ardor damped, your strength exhausted and your treasure spent, other chieftains will spring up to take advantage of your extremity. Then no man, however wise, will be able to avert the consequences that must ensue.

5. Thus, though we have heard of stupid haste in war, cleverness has never been seen associated with long delays.

6. There is no instance of a country having benefited from prolonged warfare.

7. It is only one who is thoroughly acquainted with the evils of war that can thoroughly understand the profitable way of carrying it on.

8. The skillful soldier does not raise a second levy, neither are his supply-wagons loaded more than twice.

---

[5] As seen in the ensuing lines, Sun Tzu warned against the drain of extended campaigns or drawn-out occupations. Compare to chapter VI in the *Tao Te Ching*: "The good man wins a victory and then stops; he will not go on to acts of violence." Also in that chapter: "Where troops have been quartered, brambles and thorns spring up. In the track of great armies there must follow lean years."

9. Bring war material with you from home, but forage on the enemy. Thus the army will have food enough for its needs.[6]

10. Poverty of the State exchequer causes an army to be maintained by contributions from a distance. Contributing to maintain an army at a distance causes the people to be impoverished.

11. On the other hand, the proximity of an army causes prices to go up; and high prices cause the people's substance to be drained away.

12. When their substance is drained away, the peasantry will be afflicted by heavy exactions.

13,14. With this loss of substance and exhaustion of strength, the homes of the people will be stripped bare, and three-tenths of their income will be dissipated; while government expenses for broken chariots, worn-out horses, breast-plates and helmets, bows and arrows, spears and shields, protective mantles, draught-oxen and heavy wagons, will amount to four-tenths of its total revenue.

---

[6] Sun Tzu thought it vital to "live off the land"—no army or exploratory mission can possibly bring all of its supplies with it. Also, supply lines may get disrupted. Be prepared to supplement your supplies from the territory you enter.

15. Hence a wise general makes a point of foraging on the enemy. One cartload of the enemy's provisions is equivalent to twenty of one's own, and likewise a single picul of his provender is equivalent to twenty from one's own store.

16. Now in order to kill the enemy, our men must be roused to anger; that there may be advantage from defeating the enemy, they must have their rewards.[7]

17. Therefore in chariot fighting, when ten or more chariots have been taken, those should be rewarded who took the first. Our own flags should be substituted for those of the enemy, and the chariots mingled and used in conjunction with ours. The captured soldiers should be kindly treated and kept.

18. This is called, using the conquered foe to augment one's own strength.

19. In war, then, let your great object be victory, not lengthy campaigns.

---

[7] Although Sun Tzu warns against anger as in a commander, he is not above using it as a tactical goad among troops or adversaries. Also, before looking for strict consistency in his statements it is worth noting from chapter VI in the *Tao Te Ching*: "The truest sayings are paradoxical."

20. Thus it may be known that the leader of armies is the arbiter of the people's fate, the man on whom it depends whether the nation shall be in peace or in peril.

III.

Attack By Stratagem

1. Sun Tzu said: In the practical art of war, the best thing of all is to take the enemy's country whole and intact; to shatter and destroy it is not so good. So, too, it is better to recapture an army entire than to destroy it, to capture a regiment, a detachment or a company entire than to destroy them.[8]

2. Hence to fight and conquer in all your battles is not supreme excellence; supreme excellence consists in breaking the enemy's resistance without fighting.[9]

3. Thus the highest form of generalship is to balk the enemy's plans; the next best is to prevent the junc-

---

[8] As alluded earlier, Sun Tzu believed in repurposing the resources of the enemy for your own means.

[9] This is another of Sun Tzu's key principles: to win without fighting. Strength and foreknowledge ideally make combat unnecessary; victory is won by outmaneuvering or outflanking the enemy and thus breaking his nerve or resolve. A display of overwhelming might will also deter your adversary. There is a subtler dimension to this point: dominant nature, composed of the Way, knowledge, and preparation create natural advantage. See chapter IV of the *Tao Te Ching*: "The greatest conquerors are those who overcome their enemies without strife."

tion of the enemy's forces; the next in order is to attack the enemy's army in the field; and the worst policy of all is to besiege walled cities.

4. The rule is, not to besiege walled cities if it can possibly be avoided. The preparation of mantlets,[10] movable shelters, and various implements of war, will take up three whole months; and the piling up of mounds over against the walls will take three months more.

5. The general, unable to control his irritation, will launch his men to the assault like swarming ants, with the result that one-third of his men are slain, while the town still remains untaken. Such are the disastrous effects of a siege.

6. Therefore the skillful leader subdues the enemy's troops without any fighting; he captures their cities without laying siege to them; he overthrows their kingdom without lengthy operations in the field.

7. With his forces intact he will dispute the mastery of the Empire, and thus, without losing a man, his triumph will be complete. This is the method of attacking by stratagem.

---

[10] These are screens or shields.

8. It is the rule in war, if our forces are ten to the enemy's one, to surround him; if five to one, to attack him; if twice as numerous, to divide our army into two.

9. If equally matched, we can offer battle; if slightly inferior in numbers, we can avoid the enemy; if quite unequal in every way, we can flee from him.

10. Hence, though an obstinate fight may be made by a small force, in the end it must be captured by the larger force.

11. Now the general is the bulwark of the State; if the bulwark is complete at all points; the State will be strong; if the bulwark is defective, the State will be weak.

12. There are three ways in which a ruler can bring misfortune upon his army:

13. (1) By commanding the army to advance or to retreat, being ignorant of the fact that it cannot obey. This is called hobbling the army.

14. (2) By attempting to govern an army in the same way as he administers a kingdom, being ignorant of

the conditions which obtain in an army. This causes restlessness in the soldier's minds.

15. (3) By employing the officers of his army without discrimination, through ignorance of the military principle of adaptation to circumstances. This shakes the confidence of the soldiers.

16. But when the army is restless and distrustful, trouble is sure to come from the other feudal princes. This is simply bringing anarchy into the army, and flinging victory away.

17. Thus we may know that there are five essentials for victory:
    (1) He will win who knows when to fight and when not to fight.
    (2) He will win who knows how to handle both superior and inferior forces.
    (3) He will win whose army is animated by the same spirit throughout all its ranks.
    (4) He will win who, prepared himself, waits to take the enemy unprepared.
    (5) He will win who has military capacity and is not interfered with by the sovereign.

18. Hence the saying: If you know the enemy and know yourself, you need not fear the result of a hundred battles. If you know yourself but not the enemy, for every victory gained you will also suffer a defeat. If you know neither the enemy nor yourself, you will succumb in every battle.

IV.

Tactical Dispositions

1. Sun Tzu said: The good fighters of old first put themselves beyond the possibility of defeat, and then waited for an opportunity of defeating the enemy.

2. To secure ourselves against defeat lies in our own hands, but the opportunity of defeating the enemy is provided by the enemy himself.

3. Thus the good fighter is able to secure himself against defeat, but cannot make certain of defeating the enemy.

4. Hence the saying: One may *know* how to conquer without being able to *do* it.[11]

5. Security against defeat implies defensive tactics; ability to defeat the enemy means taking the offensive.

---

[11] This is natural law: where two parties are involved the outcome depends on the actions of both.

6. Standing on the defensive indicates insufficient strength; attacking, a superabundance of strength.

7. The general who is skilled in defense hides in the most secret recesses of the earth; he who is skilled in attack flashes forth from the topmost heights of heaven. Thus on the one hand we have ability to protect ourselves; on the other, a victory that is complete.

8. To see victory only when it is within the ken of the common herd is not the acme of excellence.

9. Neither is it the acme of excellence if you fight and conquer and the whole Empire says, "Well done!"[12]

10. To lift an autumn hair is no sign of great strength; to see the sun and moon is no sign of sharp sight; to hear the noise of thunder is no sign of a quick ear.[13]

11. What the ancients called a clever fighter is one who not only wins, but excels in winning with ease.

---

[12] See also verse 12. The great warrior does his work without ever being apparent. His victory is so natural that it is not even noticed.

[13] Do not credit yourself for ordinary means and methods; seek impeccable means. No one is rewarded for just doing his job.

12. Hence his victories bring him neither reputation for wisdom nor credit for courage.[14]

13. He wins his battles by making no mistakes. Making no mistakes is what establishes the certainty of victory, for it means conquering an enemy that is already defeated.

14. Hence the skillful fighter puts himself into a position which makes defeat impossible, and does not miss the moment for defeating the enemy.

15. Thus it is that in war the victorious strategist only seeks battle after the victory has been won, whereas he who is destined to defeat first fights and afterwards looks for victory.

16. The consummate leader cultivates the moral law, and strictly adheres to method and discipline; thus it is in his power to control success.[15]

---

[14] This is one of Sun Tzu's subtlest and most overlooked points. The greatest commander prevails with such ease, possibly without fighting or casualties at all, that he is not the subject of "glory." His victories appear so natural that they go unnoticed. The commander who seeks glory is liable to risk, extended campaigns, and massive loss.

[15] It is useful to note that Sun Tzu adheres not to inspiration, which can come and go, but to "method and discipline," where are permanent. Compare to chapter VI in the *Tao Te Ching*: "Winning, he boasteth not; he will not triumph; he shows no arrogance. He wins because he cannot choose [i.e., it is natural]; after his victory he will not be overbearing."

17. In respect of military method, we have, firstly, Measurement; secondly, Estimation of quantity; thirdly, Calculation; fourthly, Balancing of chances; fifthly, Victory.

18. Measurement owes its existence to Earth; Estimation of quantity to Measurement; Calculation to Estimation of quantity; Balancing of chances to Calculation; and Victory to Balancing of chances.

19. A victorious army opposed to a routed one, is as a pound's weight placed in the scale against a single grain.

20. The onrush of a conquering force is like the bursting of pent-up waters into a chasm a thousand fathoms deep.[16]

---

[16] See chapter VI, verse 29, for an expansion on the qualities of water and warfare.

V.

Energy

1. Sun Tzu said: The control of a large force is the same principle as the control of a few men: it is merely a question of dividing up their numbers.

2. Fighting with a large army under your command is nowise different from fighting with a small one: it is merely a question of instituting signs and signals.

3. To ensure that your whole host may withstand the brunt of the enemy's attack and remain unshaken— this is affected by maneuvers direct and indirect.

4. That the impact of your army may be like a grindstone dashed against an egg—this is effected by the science of weak points and strong.

5. In all fighting, the direct method may be used for joining battle, but indirect methods will be needed in order to secure victory.

6. Indirect tactics, efficiently applied, are inexhaustible as Heaven and Earth, unending as the flow of rivers and streams; like the sun and moon, they end but to begin anew; like the four seasons, they pass away to return once more.[17]

7. There are not more than five musical notes, yet the combinations of these five give rise to more melodies than can ever be heard.

8. There are not more than five primary colors (blue, yellow, red, white, and black), yet in combination they produce more hues than can ever been seen.

9. There are not more than five cardinal tastes (sour, acrid, salt, sweet, bitter), yet combinations of them yield more flavors than can ever be tasted.

10. In battle, there are not more than two methods of attack—the direct and the indirect; yet these two in combination give rise to an endless series of maneuvers.

---

[17] This precept should be read and considered carefully with the one immediately preceding it. In Sun Tzu's philosophy, principles of flexibility are vital. Combinations are limitless. A commander should never grow comfortable with any one tactic. Tactics may be repeated—but be cautious: losses often result from the reapplication of a tactic that formerly brought victory but is unsuited to a new challenge.

11. The direct and the indirect lead on to each other in turn. It is like moving in a circle—you never come to an end. Who can exhaust the possibilities of their combination?

12. The onset of troops is like the rush of a torrent which will even roll stones along in its course.[18]

13. The quality of decision is like the well-timed swoop of a falcon which enables it to strike and destroy its victim.

14. Therefore the good fighter will be terrible in his onset, and prompt in his decision.

15. Energy may be likened to the bending of a crossbow; decision, to the releasing of a trigger.

16. Amid the turmoil and tumult of battle, there may be seeming disorder and yet no real disorder at all; amid confusion and chaos, your array may be without head or tail, yet it will be proof against defeat.

---

[18] Here and in the immediately following lines Sun Tzu is teaching that once an attack is decided on it must be carried out with absolute decisiveness, dedication, and ferocity. Otherwise it is better not to attack.

17. Simulated disorder postulates perfect discipline, simulated fear postulates courage; simulated weakness postulates strength.

18. Hiding order beneath the cloak of disorder is simply a question of subdivision; concealing courage under a show of timidity presupposes a fund of latent energy; masking strength with weakness is to be effected by tactical dispositions.

19. Thus one who is skillful at keeping the enemy on the move maintains deceitful appearances, according to which the enemy will act. He sacrifices something, that the enemy may snatch at it.

20. By holding out baits, he keeps him on the march; then with a body of picked men he lies in wait for him.

21. The clever combatant looks to the effect of combined energy, and does not require too much from individuals. Hence his ability to pick out the right men and utilize combined energy.[19]

22. When he utilizes combined energy, his fighting men become as it were like unto rolling logs or stones.

---

[19] Sun Tzu is saying that you must not over-rely on any one person or factor.

For it is the nature of a log or stone to remain motionless on level ground, and to move when on a slope; if four-cornered, to come to a standstill, but if round-shaped, to go rolling down.

23. Thus the energy developed by good fighting men is as the momentum of a round stone rolled down a mountain thousands of feet in height. So much on the subject of energy.

VI.

Weak Points and Strong

1. Sun Tzu said: Whoever is first in the field and awaits the coming of the enemy, will be fresh for the fight; whoever is second in the field and has to hasten to battle will arrive exhausted.[20]

2. Therefore the clever combatant imposes his will on the enemy, but does not allow the enemy's will to be imposed on him.

3. By holding out advantages to him, he can cause the enemy to approach of his own accord; or, by inflicting damage, he can make it impossible for the enemy to draw near.

4. If the enemy is taking his ease, he can harass him; if well supplied with food, he can starve him out; if quietly encamped, he can force him to move.

---

[20] This is one of Sun Tzu's most practical lessons: always arrive first.

5. Appear at points which the enemy must hasten to defend; march swiftly to places where you are not expected.

6. An army may march great distances without distress, if it marches through country where the enemy is not.

7. You can be sure of succeeding in your attacks if you only attack places which are undefended. You can ensure the safety of your defense if you only hold positions that cannot be attacked.

8. Hence that general is skillful in attack whose opponent does not know what to defend; and he is skillful in defense whose opponent does not know what to attack.

9. O divine art of subtlety and secrecy! Through you we learn to be invisible, through you inaudible; and hence we can hold the enemy's fate in our hands.

10. You may advance and be absolutely irresistible, if you make for the enemy's weak points; you may retire and be safe from pursuit if your movements are more rapid than those of the enemy.

11. If we wish to fight, the enemy can be forced to an engagement even though he be sheltered behind a high rampart and a deep ditch. All we need do is attack some other place that he will be obliged to relieve.

12. If we do not wish to fight, we can prevent the enemy from engaging us even though the lines of our encampment be merely traced out on the ground. All we need do is to throw something odd and unaccountable in his way.

13. By discovering the enemy's dispositions and remaining invisible ourselves, we can keep our forces concentrated, while the enemy's must be divided.

14. We can form a single united body, while the enemy must split up into fractions. Hence there will be a whole pitted against separate parts of a whole, which means that we shall be many to the enemy's few.

15. And if we are able thus to attack an inferior force with a superior one, our opponents will be in dire straits.

16. The spot where we intend to fight must not be made known; for then the enemy will have to prepare against a possible attack at several different points; and his forces being thus distributed in many directions, the numbers we shall have to face at any given point will be proportionately few.

17. For should the enemy strengthen his van, he will weaken his rear; should he strengthen his rear, he will weaken his van; should he strengthen his left, he will weaken his right; should he strengthen his right, he will weaken his left. If he sends reinforcements everywhere, he will everywhere be weak.

18. Numerical weakness comes from having to prepare against possible attacks; numerical strength, from compelling our adversary to make these preparations against us.

19. Knowing the place and the time of the coming battle, we may concentrate from the greatest distances in order to fight.

20. But if neither time nor place be known, then the left wing will be impotent to succor the right, the right equally impotent to succor the left, the van unable to relieve the rear, or the rear to support

the van. How much more so if the furthest portions of the army are anything under a hundred *li* apart, and even the nearest are separated by several *li*!

21. Though according to my estimate the soldiers of Yueh exceed our own in number, that shall advantage them nothing in the matter of victory. I say then that victory can be achieved.

22. Though the enemy be stronger in numbers, we may prevent him from fighting. Scheme so as to discover his plans and the likelihood of their success.

23. Rouse him, and learn the principle of his activity or inactivity. Force him to reveal himself, so as to find out his vulnerable spots.

24. Carefully compare the opposing army with your own, so that you may know where strength is superabundant and where it is deficient.

25. In making tactical dispositions, the highest pitch you can attain is to conceal them; conceal your dispositions, and you will be safe from the prying of the subtlest spies, from the machinations of the wisest brains.

26. How victory may be produced for them out of the enemy's own tactics—that is what the multitude cannot comprehend.

27. All men can see the tactics whereby I conquer, but what none can see is the strategy out of which victory is evolved.

28. Do not repeat the tactics which have gained you one victory, but let your methods be regulated by the infinite variety of circumstances.

29. Military tactics are like unto water; for water in its natural course runs away from high places and hastens downwards.[21]

30. So in war, the way is to avoid what is strong and to strike at what is weak.

---

[21] Take careful note of all of Sun Tzu's references to water. Water is humble and subtle. It dwells at low places. (On a related note, see chapter VIII in the *Tao Te Ching*: "He who raises himself on tiptoe cannot stand firm; he who stretches his legs wide apart cannot walk.") But when in a torrent or onrush, water proves irresistible. Like water, you must go unnoticed when observing your enemy. But when attacking you must strike overwhelmingly, crashing like a wave through his defenses at their weakest point. Also note line 20 in chapter IV: "The onrush of a conquering force is like the bursting of pent-up waters into a chasm a thousand fathoms deep." And in the *Tao Te Ching*, chapter II: "The highest goodness is like water, for water is excellent in benefiting all things, and it does not strive. It occupies the lowest place, which men abhor. And therefore it is near akin to Tao."

31. Water shapes its course according to the nature of the ground over which it flows; the soldier works out his victory in relation to the foe whom he is facing.[22]

32. Therefore, just as water retains no constant shape, so in warfare there are no constant conditions.

33. He who can modify his tactics in relation to his opponent and thereby succeed in winning, may be called a heaven-born captain.

34. The five elements (water, fire, wood, metal, earth) are not always equally predominant; the four seasons make way for each other in turn. There are short days and long; the moon has its periods of waning and waxing.

---

[22] Sun Tzu is counseling flexibility, morphing, and ready response to changed circumstances. Do not be rigid.

VII.

Maneuvering

1. Sun Tzu said: In war, the general receives his commands from the sovereign.

2. Having collected an army and concentrated his forces, he must blend and harmonize the different elements thereof before pitching his camp.

3. After that, comes tactical maneuvering, than which there is nothing more difficult. The difficulty of tactical maneuvering consists in turning the devious into the direct, and misfortune into gain.

4. Thus, to take a long and circuitous route, after enticing the enemy out of the way, and though starting after him, to contrive to reach the goal before him, shows knowledge of the artifice of *deviation*.

5. Maneuvering with an army is advantageous; with an undisciplined multitude, most dangerous.

6. If you set a fully equipped army in march in order to snatch an advantage, the chances are that you will be too late. On the other hand, to detach a flying column for the purpose involves the sacrifice of its baggage and stores.

7. Thus, if you order your men to roll up their buff-coats, and make forced marches without halting day or night, covering double the usual distance at a stretch, doing a hundred *li* in order to wrest an advantage, the leaders of all your three divisions will fall into the hands of the enemy.

8. The stronger men will be in front, the jaded ones will fall behind, and on this plan only one-tenth of your army will reach its destination.

9. If you march fifty *li* in order to outmaneuver the enemy, you will lose the leader of your first division, and only half your force will reach the goal.

10. If you march thirty *li* with the same object, two-thirds of your army will arrive.

11. We may take it then that an army without its baggage-train is lost; without provisions it is lost; without bases of supply it is lost.

12. We cannot enter into alliances until we are acquainted with the designs of our neighbors.

13. We are not fit to lead an army on the march unless we are familiar with the face of the country—its mountains and forests, its pitfalls and precipices, its marshes and swamps.

14. We shall be unable to turn natural advantage to account unless we make use of local guides.

15. In war, practice dissimulation, and you will succeed.

16. Whether to concentrate or to divide your troops, must be decided by circumstances.

17. Let your rapidity be that of the wind, your compactness that of the forest.

18. In raiding and plundering be like fire, is immovability like a mountain.

19. Let your plans be dark and impenetrable as night, and when you move, fall like a thunderbolt.

20. When you plunder a countryside, let the spoil be divided amongst your men; when you capture new

territory, cut it up into allotments for the benefit of the soldiery.

21. Ponder and deliberate before you make a move.

22. He will conquer who has learnt the artifice of deviation. Such is the art of maneuvering.

23. The Book of Army Management says: On the field of battle, the spoken word does not carry far enough: hence the institution of gongs and drums. Nor can ordinary objects be seen clearly enough: hence the institution of banners and flags.

24. Gongs and drums, banners and flags, are means whereby the ears and eyes of the host may be focused on one particular point.

25. The host thus forming a single united body, is it impossible either for the brave to advance alone, or for the cowardly to retreat alone. This is the art of handling large masses of men.

26. In night-fighting, then, make much use of signal-fires and drums, and in fighting by day, of flags and banners, as a means of influencing the ears and eyes of your army.

27. A whole army may be robbed of its spirit; a commander-in-chief may be robbed of his presence of mind.

28. Now a soldier's spirit is keenest in the morning; by noonday it has begun to flag; and in the evening, his mind is bent only on returning to camp.

29. A clever general, therefore, avoids an army when its spirit is keen, but attacks it when it is sluggish and inclined to return. This is the art of studying moods.

30. Disciplined and calm, to await the appearance of disorder and hubbub amongst the enemy: this is the art of retaining self-possession.

31. To be near the goal while the enemy is still far from it, to wait at ease while the enemy is toiling and struggling, to be well-fed while the enemy is famished: this is the art of husbanding one's strength.

32. To refrain from intercepting an enemy whose banners are in perfect order, to refrain from attacking an army drawn up in calm and confident array: this is the art of studying circumstances.

33. It is a military axiom not to advance uphill against the enemy, nor to oppose him when he comes downhill.

34. Do not pursue an enemy who simulates flight; do not attack soldiers whose temper is keen.

35. Do not swallow bait offered by the enemy. Do not interfere with an army that is returning home.

36. When you surround an army, leave an outlet free. Do not press a desperate foe too hard.[23]

37. Such is the art of warfare.

---

[23] As noted in the introduction, Sun Tzu is teaching that by pressing a desperate foe and leaving him no way out, you ensure that he will fight to the death, with severe consequences on both sides. Giles observes that leaving an "outlet free" may also be a matter of strategic deception. He quotes Chinese poet Du Mu (803–852 A.D.) that the aim is "to make him believe that there is a road to safety and thus prevent his fighting with the courage of despair."

VIII.

Variation of Tactics

1. Sun Tzu said: In war, the general receives his commands from the sovereign, collects his army and concentrates his forces

2. When in difficult country, do not encamp. In country where high roads intersect, join hands with your allies. Do not linger in dangerously isolated positions. In hemmed-in situations, you must resort to stratagem. In desperate position, you must fight.

3. There are roads which must not be followed, armies which must be not attacked, towns which must be besieged, positions which must not be contested, commands of the sovereign which must not be obeyed.

4. The general who thoroughly understands the advantages that accompany variation of tactics knows how to handle his troops.

5. The general who does not understand these, may be well acquainted with the configuration of the country, yet he will not be able to turn his knowledge to practical account.

6. So, the student of war who is unversed in the art of war of varying his plans, even though he be acquainted with the Five Advantages, will fail to make the best use of his men.[24]

7. Hence in the wise leader's plans, considerations of advantage and of disadvantage will be blended together.

8. If our expectation of advantage be tempered in this way, we may succeed in accomplishing the essential part of our schemes.

9. If, on the other hand, in the midst of difficulties we are always ready to seize an advantage, we may extricate ourselves from misfortune.

10. Reduce the hostile chiefs by inflicting damage on them; and make trouble for them, and keep them

---

[24] For the "Five Advantages," see Sun Tzu's note on the "five essentials for victory" in chapter III.

constantly engaged; hold out specious allurements, and make them rush to any given point.

11. The art of war teaches us to rely not on the likelihood of the enemy's not coming, but on our own readiness to receive him; not on the chance of his not attacking, but rather on the fact that we have made our position unassailable.

12. There are five dangerous faults which may affect a general:
    (1) Recklessness, which leads to destruction;
    (2) cowardice, which leads to capture;
    (3) a hasty temper, which can be provoked by insults;
    (4) a delicacy of honor which is sensitive to shame;
    (5) over-solicitude for his men, which exposes him to worry and trouble.

13. These are the five besetting sins of a general, ruinous to the conduct of war.

14. When an army is overthrown and its leader slain, the cause will surely be found among these five dangerous faults. Let them be a subject of meditation.

IX.

The Army On the March

1. Sun Tzu said: We come now to the question of encamping the army, and observing signs of the enemy. Pass quickly over mountains, and keep in the neighborhood of valleys.

2. Camp in high places, facing the sun. Do not climb heights in order to fight. So much for mountain warfare.

3. After crossing a river, you should get far away from it.

4. When an invading force crosses a river in its onward march, do not advance to meet it in mid-stream. It will be best to let half the army get across, and then deliver your attack.

5. If you are anxious to fight, you should not go to meet the invader near a river which he has to cross.

6. Moor your craft higher up than the enemy, and facing the sun. Do not move up-stream to meet the enemy. So much for river warfare.

7. In crossing salt-marshes, your sole concern should be to get over them quickly, without any delay.

8. If forced to fight in a salt-marsh, you should have water and grass near you, and get your back to a clump of trees. So much for operations in salt-marshes.

9. In dry, level country, take up an easily accessible position with rising ground to your right and on your rear, so that the danger may be in front, and safety lie behind. So much for campaigning in flat country.

10. These are the four useful branches of military knowledge which enabled the Yellow Emperor to vanquish four several sovereigns.

11. All armies prefer high ground to low and sunny places to dark.

12. If you are careful of your men, and camp on hard ground, the army will be free from disease of every kind, and this will spell victory.

13. When you come to a hill or a bank, occupy the sunny side, with the slope on your right rear. Thus you will at once act for the benefit of your soldiers and utilize the natural advantages of the ground.

14. When, in consequence of heavy rains up-country, a river which you wish to ford is swollen and flecked with foam, you must wait until it subsides.

15. Country in which there are precipitous cliffs with torrents running between, deep natural hollows, confined places, tangled thickets, quagmires and crevasses, should be left with all possible speed and not approached.

16. While we keep away from such places, we should get the enemy to approach them; while we face them, we should let the enemy have them on his rear.

17. If in the neighborhood of your camp there should be any hilly country, ponds surrounded by aquatic grass, hollow basins filled with reeds, or woods with thick undergrowth, they must be carefully routed out and searched; for these are places where men in ambush or insidious spies are likely to be lurking.

18. When the enemy is close at hand and remains quiet, he is relying on the natural strength of his position.

19. When he keeps aloof and tries to provoke a battle, he is anxious for the other side to advance.

20. If his place of encampment is easy of access, he is tendering a bait.

21. Movement amongst the trees of a forest shows that the enemy is advancing. The appearance of a number of screens in the midst of thick grass means that the enemy wants to make us suspicious.

22. The rising of birds in their flight is the sign of an ambuscade. Startled beasts indicate that a sudden attack is coming.

23. When there is dust rising in a high column, it is the sign of chariots advancing; when the dust is low, but spread over a wide area, it betokens the approach of infantry. When it branches out in different directions, it shows that parties have been sent to collect firewood. A few clouds of dust moving to and fro signify that the army is encamping.

24. Humble words and increased preparations are signs that the enemy is about to advance. Violent language and driving forward as if to the attack are signs that he will retreat.

25. When the light chariots come out first and take up a position on the wings, it is a sign that the enemy is forming for battle.

26. Peace proposals unaccompanied by a sworn covenant indicate a plot.

27. When there is much running about and the soldiers fall into rank, it means that the critical moment has come.

28. When some are seen advancing and some retreating, it is a lure.

29. When the soldiers stand leaning on their spears, they are faint from want of food.

30. If those who are sent to draw water begin by drinking themselves, the army is suffering from thirst.

31. If the enemy sees an advantage to be gained and makes no effort to secure it, the soldiers are exhausted.

32. If birds gather on any spot, it is unoccupied. Clamor by night betokens nervousness.

33. If there is disturbance in the camp, the general's authority is weak. If the banners and flags are shifted about, sedition is afoot. If the officers are angry, it means that the men are weary.

34. When an army feeds its horses with grain and kills its cattle for food, and when the men do not hang their cooking-pots over the camp-fires, showing that they will not return to their tents, you may know that they are determined to fight to the death.[25]

35. The sight of men whispering together in small knots or speaking in subdued tones points to disaffection amongst the rank and file.

36. Too frequent rewards signify that the enemy is at the end of his resources; too many punishments betray a condition of dire distress.

---

[25] Men eat grain; horses eat grass. Hence, the slaying of cattle means a preparation for the end.

37. To begin by bluster, but afterwards to take fright at the enemy's numbers, shows a supreme lack of intelligence.

38. When envoys are sent with compliments in their mouths, it is a sign that the enemy wishes for a truce.

39. If the enemy's troops march up angrily and remain facing ours for a long time without either joining battle or taking themselves off again, the situation is one that demands great vigilance and circum-spection.

40. If our troops are no more in number than the enemy, that is amply sufficient; it only means that no direct attack can be made. What we can do is simply to concentrate all our available strength, keep a close watch on the enemy, and obtain reinforcements.

41. He who exercises no forethought but makes light of his opponents is sure to be captured by them.

42. If soldiers are punished before they have grown attached to you, they will not prove submissive; and, unless submissive, then will be practically use-less. If, when the soldiers have become attached to

you, punishments are not enforced, they will still be useless.

43. Therefore soldiers must be treated in the first instance with humanity, but kept under control by means of iron discipline. This is a certain road to victory.

44. If in training soldiers commands are habitually enforced, the army will be well-disciplined; if not, its discipline will be bad.

45. If a general shows confidence in his men but always insists on his orders being obeyed, the gain will be mutual.

X.

Terrain

1. Sun Tzu said: We may distinguish six kinds of terrain, to wit:
   (1) Accessible ground;
   (2) entangling ground;
   (3) temporizing ground;
   (4) narrow passes;
   (5) precipitous heights;
   (6) positions at a great distance from the enemy.

2. Ground which can be freely traversed by both sides is called accessible.

3. With regard to ground of this nature, be before the enemy in occupying the raised and sunny spots, and carefully guard your line of supplies. Then you will be able to fight with advantage.

4. Ground which can be abandoned but is hard to re-occupy is called entangling.

5. From a position of this sort, if the enemy is unprepared, you may sally forth and defeat him. But if the enemy is prepared for your coming, and you fail to defeat him, then, return being impossible, disaster will ensue.

6. When the position is such that neither side will gain by making the first move, it is called *temporizing* ground.

7. In a position of this sort, even though the enemy should offer us an attractive bait, it will be advisable not to stir forth, but rather to retreat, thus enticing the enemy in his turn; then, when part of his army has come out, we may deliver our attack with advantage.

8. With regard to *narrow passes*, if you can occupy them first, let them be strongly garrisoned and await the advent of the enemy.

9. Should the army forestall you in occupying a pass, do not go after him if the pass is fully garrisoned, but only if it is weakly garrisoned.

10. With regard to *precipitous heights*, if you are beforehand with your adversary, you should occupy the

raised and sunny spots, and there wait for him to come up.

11. If the enemy has occupied them before you, do not follow him, but retreat and try to entice him away.

12. If you are situated at a great distance from the enemy, and the strength of the two armies is equal, it is not easy to provoke a battle, and fighting will be to your disadvantage.

13. These six are the principles connected with Earth. The general who has attained a responsible post must be careful to study them.

14. Now an army is exposed to six several calamities, not arising from natural causes, but from faults for which the general is responsible. These are:
(1) Flight;
(2) insubordination;
(3) collapse;
(4) ruin;
(5) disorganization;
(6) rout.

15. Other conditions being equal, if one force is hurled against another ten times its size, the result will be the *flight* of the former.

16. When the common soldiers are too strong and their officers too weak, the result is *insubordination*. When the officers are too strong and the common soldiers too weak, the result is *collapse*.

17. When the higher officers are angry and insubordinate, and on meeting the enemy give battle on their own account from a feeling of resentment, before the commander-in-chief can tell whether or not he is in a position to fight, the result is ruin.

18. When the general is weak and without authority; when his orders are not clear and distinct; when there are no fixes duties assigned to officers and men, and the ranks are formed in a slovenly haphazard manner, the result is utter *disorganization*.

19. When a general, unable to estimate the enemy's strength, allows an inferior force to engage a larger one, or hurls a weak detachment against a powerful one, and neglects to place picked soldiers in the front rank, the result must be *rout*.

20. These are six ways of courting defeat, which must be carefully noted by the general who has attained a responsible post.

21. The natural formation of the country is the soldier's best ally; but a power of estimating the adversary, of controlling the forces of victory, and of shrewdly calculating difficulties, dangers and distances, constitutes the test of a great general.

22. He who knows these things, and in fighting puts his knowledge into practice, will win his battles. He who knows them not, nor practices them, will surely be defeated.

23. If fighting is sure to result in victory, then you must fight, even though the ruler forbid it; if fighting will not result in victory, then you must not fight even at the ruler's bidding.

24. The general who advances without coveting fame and retreats without fearing disgrace, whose only thought is to protect his country and do good service for his sovereign, is the jewel of the kingdom.

25. Regard your soldiers as your children, and they will follow you into the deepest valleys; look upon them

as your own beloved sons, and they will stand by
you even unto death.

26. If, however, you are indulgent, but unable to make
your authority felt; kind-hearted, but unable to
enforce your commands; and incapable, moreover,
of quelling disorder: then your soldiers must be
likened to spoilt children; they are useless for any
practical purpose.

27. If we know that our own men are in a condition to
attack, but are unaware that the enemy is not open
to attack, we have gone only halfway towards victory.

28. If we know that the enemy is open to attack, but are
unaware that our own men are not in a condition to
attack, we have gone only halfway towards victory.

29. If we know that the enemy is open to attack, and
also know that our men are in a condition to attack,
but are unaware that the nature of the ground
makes fighting impracticable, we have still gone
only halfway towards victory.

30. Hence the experienced soldier, once in motion, is
never bewildered; once he has broken camp, he is
never at a loss.

31. Hence the saying: If you know the enemy and know yourself, your victory will not stand in doubt; if you know Heaven and know Earth, you may make your victory complete.

XI.

The Nine Situations

1. Sun Tzu said: The art of war recognizes nine varieties of ground:

    (1) Dispersive ground;

    (2) facile ground;

    (3) contentious ground;

    (4) open ground;

    (5) ground of intersecting highways;

    (6) serious ground;

    (7) difficult ground;

    (8) hemmed-in ground;

    (9) desperate ground.

2. When a chieftain is fighting in his own territory, it is dispersive ground.

3. When he has penetrated into hostile territory, but to no great distance, it is facile ground.

4. Ground the possession of which imports great advantage to either side, is contentious ground.

5. Ground on which each side has liberty of movement is open ground.

6. Ground which forms the key to three contiguous states, so that he who occupies it first has most of the Empire at his command, is a ground of intersecting highways.

7. When an army has penetrated into the heart of a hostile country, leaving a number of fortified cities in its rear, it is serious ground.

8. Mountain forests, rugged steeps, marshes and fens—all country that is hard to traverse: this is difficult ground.

9. Ground which is reached through narrow gorges, and from which we can only retire by tortuous paths, so that a small number of the enemy would suffice to crush a large body of our men: this is hemmed in ground.

10. Ground on which we can only be saved from destruction by fighting without delay, is desperate ground.

11. On dispersive ground, therefore, fight not. On facile ground, halt not. On contentious ground, attack not.

12. On open ground, do not try to block the enemy's way. On the ground of intersecting highways, join hands with your allies.

13. On serious ground, gather in plunder. In difficult ground, keep steadily on the march.

14. On hemmed-in ground, resort to stratagem. On desperate ground, fight.

15. Those who were called skillful leaders of old knew how to drive a wedge between the enemy's front and rear; to prevent co-operation between his large and small divisions; to hinder the good troops from rescuing the bad, the officers from rallying their men.

16. When the enemy's men were united, they managed to keep them in disorder.

17. When it was to their advantage, they made a forward move; when otherwise, they stopped still.

18. If asked how to cope with a great host of the enemy in orderly array and on the point of marching to the attack, I should say: "Begin by seizing something which your opponent holds dear; then he will be amenable to your will."

19. Rapidity is the essence of war: take advantage of the enemy's unreadiness, make your way by unexpected routes, and attack unguarded spots.

20. The following are the principles to be observed by an invading force: The further you penetrate into a country, the greater will be the solidarity of your troops, and thus the defenders will not prevail against you.

21. Make forays in fertile country in order to supply your army with food.

22. Carefully study the well-being of your men, and do not overtax them. Concentrate your energy and hoard your strength. Keep your army continually on the move, and devise unfathomable plans.

23. Throw your soldiers into positions whence there is no escape, and they will prefer death to flight. If they will face death, there is nothing they may not achieve. Officers and men alike will put forth their uttermost strength.

24. Soldiers when in desperate straits lose the sense of fear. If there is no place of refuge, they will stand firm. If they are in hostile country, they will show

a stubborn front. If there is no help for it, they will fight hard.

25. Thus, without waiting to be marshaled, the soldiers will be constantly on the *qui vive*;[26] without waiting to be asked, they will do your will; without restrictions, they will be faithful; without giving orders, they can be trusted.

26. Prohibit the taking of omens, and do away with superstitious doubts. Then, until death itself comes, no calamity need be feared.

27. If our soldiers are not overburdened with money, it is not because they have a distaste for riches; if their lives are not unduly long, it is not because they are disinclined to longevity.

28. On the day they are ordered out to battle, your soldiers may weep, those sitting up bedewing their garments, and those lying down letting the tears run down their cheeks. But let them once be brought to bay, and they will display the courage of a Chu or a Kuei.[27]

---

[26] I.e., on alert.

[27] Sun Tzu refers here to the legendary Chinese warriors Chuan Chu (c. 6th century BC) and Ts`ao Kuei (c. 7th century BC). He is saying that if you leave your warriors with no way out they will fight with ferocity.

29. The skillful tactician may be likened to the *shuai-jan*.[28] Now the *shuai-jan* is a snake that is found in the Ch'ang mountains. Strike at its head, and you will be attacked by its tail; strike at its tail, and you will be attacked by its head; strike at its middle, and you will be attacked by head and tail both.

30. Asked if an army can be made to imitate the *shuai-jan*, I should answer, Yes. For the men of Wu and the men of Yueh are enemies; yet if they are crossing a river in the same boat and are caught by a storm, they will come to each other's assistance just as the left hand helps the right.

31. Hence it is not enough to put one's trust in the tethering of horses, and the burying of chariot wheels in the ground.[29]

32. The principle on which to manage an army is to set up one standard of courage which all must reach.

---

[28] Sun Tzu refers here to a species of rapidly moving snake.

[29] Here and in the preceding verse, Sun Tzu is counseling to fasten your army in one place, compel your forces to depend on each other for life, and they will fight fiercely and in concert.

33. How to make the best of both strong and weak—
    that is a question involving the proper use of
    ground.

34. Thus the skillful general conducts his army just as
    though he were leading a single man, willy-nilly, by
    the hand.

35. It is the business of a general to be quiet and thus
    ensure secrecy; upright and just, and thus main-
    tain order.

36. He must be able to mystify his officers and men by
    false reports and appearances, and thus keep them
    in total ignorance.

37. By altering his arrangements and changing his
    plans, he keeps the enemy without definite knowl-
    edge. By shifting his camp and taking circuitous
    routes, he prevents the enemy from anticipating his
    purpose.

38. At the critical moment, the leader of an army acts
    like one who has climbed up a height and then
    kicks away the ladder behind him. He carries his
    men deep into hostile territory before he shows his
    hand.

39. He burns his boats and breaks his cooking-pots; like a shepherd driving a flock of sheep, he drives his men this way and that, and nothing knows whither he is going.[30]

40. To muster his host and bring it into danger: this may be termed the business of the general.

41. The different measures suited to the nine varieties of ground; the expediency of aggressive or defensive tactics; and the fundamental laws of human nature: these are things that must most certainly be studied.

42. When invading hostile territory, the general principle is, that penetrating deeply brings cohesion; penetrating but a short way means dispersion.

43. When you leave your own country behind, and take your army across neighborhood territory, you find yourself on critical ground. When there are means of communication on all four sides, the ground is one of intersecting highways.

---

[30] The reference to burning boats and breaking cooking pots is akin to the Western expression to "burn the fleet"—in other words, to eliminate any way out and thus to guarantee victory or demise. This also makes a show of determination to troops and foes.

44. When you penetrate deeply into a country, it is serious ground. When you penetrate but a little way, it is facile ground.

45. When you have the enemy's strongholds on your rear, and narrow passes in front, it is hemmed-in ground. When there is no place of refuge at all, it is desperate ground.

46. Therefore, on dispersive ground, I would inspire my men with unity of purpose. On facile ground, I would see that there is close connection between all parts of my army.

47. On contentious ground, I would hurry up my rear.

48. On open ground, I would keep a vigilant eye on my defenses. On ground of intersecting highways, I would consolidate my alliances.

49. On serious ground, I would try to ensure a continuous stream of supplies. On difficult ground, I would keep pushing on along the road.

50. On hemmed-in ground, I would block any way of retreat. On desperate ground, I would proclaim to my soldiers the hopelessness of saving their lives.

51. For it is the soldier's disposition to offer an obstinate resistance when surrounded, to fight hard when he cannot help himself, and to obey promptly when he has fallen into danger.

52. We cannot enter into alliance with neighboring princes until we are acquainted with their designs. We are not fit to lead an army on the march unless we are familiar with the face of the country—its mountains and forests, its pitfalls and precipices, its marshes and swamps. We shall be unable to turn natural advantages to account unless we make use of local guides.

53. To be ignorant of any one of the following four or five principles does not befit a warlike prince.

54. When a warlike prince attacks a powerful state, his generalship shows itself in preventing the concentration of the enemy's forces. He overawes his opponents, and their allies are prevented from joining against him.

55. Hence he does not strive to ally himself with all and sundry, nor does he foster the power of other states. He carries out his own secret designs,

keeping his antagonists in awe. Thus he is able
to capture their cities and overthrow their king-
doms.

56. Bestow rewards without regard to rule, issue orders
without regard to previous arrangements; and you
will be able to handle a whole army as though you
had to do with but a single man.

57. Confront your soldiers with the deed itself; never
let them know your design. When the outlook is
bright, bring it before their eyes; but tell them nothing when the situation is gloomy.[31]

58. Place your army in deadly peril, and it will survive;
plunge it into desperate straits, and it will come off
in safety.

59. For it is precisely when a force has fallen into harm's
way that is capable of striking a blow for victory.

60. Success in warfare is gained by carefully accommo-
dating ourselves to the enemy's purpose.

---

[31] In the first part of this principle, Sun Tzu is saying to focus troops on the goal
not on the means to the goal.

61. By persistently hanging on the enemy's flank, we shall succeed in the long run in killing the commander-in-chief.

62. This is called ability to accomplish a thing by sheer cunning.

63. On the day that you take up your command, block the frontier passes, destroy the official tallies, and stop the passage of all emissaries.

64. Be stern in the council-chamber, so that you may control the situation.

65. If the enemy leaves a door open, you must rush in.

66. Forestall your opponent by seizing what he holds dear, and subtly contrive to time his arrival on the ground.

67. Walk in the path defined by rule, and accommodate yourself to the enemy until you can fight a decisive battle.

68. At first, then, exhibit the coyness of a maiden, until the enemy gives you an opening; afterwards emulate the rapidity of a running hare, and it will be too late for the enemy to oppose you.

XII.

The Attack By Fire[32]

1. Sun Tzu said: There are five ways of attacking with fire. The first is to burn soldiers in their camp; the second is to burn stores; the third is to burn baggage trains; the fourth is to burn arsenals and magazines; the fifth is to hurl dropping fire amongst the enemy.

2. In order to carry out an attack, we must have means available. The material for raising fire should always be kept in readiness.

3. There is a proper season for making attacks with fire, and special days for starting a conflagration.

4. The proper season is when the weather is very dry; the special days are those when the moon is in the constellations of the Sieve, the Wall, the Wing or the Cross-bar; for these four are all days of rising wind.

---

[32] The tactics discussed in this chapter have one underlying theme: use the flow of nature, the essential Taoist principle.

5. In attacking with fire, one should be prepared to meet five possible developments:

6. (1) When fire breaks out inside to enemy's camp, respond at once with an attack from without.

7. (2) If there is an outbreak of fire, but the enemy's soldiers remain quiet, bide your time and do not attack.

8. (3) When the force of the flames has reached its height, follow it up with an attack, if that is practicable; if not, stay where you are.

9. (4) If it is possible to make an assault with fire from without, do not wait for it to break out within, but deliver your attack at a favorable moment.

10. (5) When you start a fire, be to windward of it. Do not attack from the leeward.

11. A wind that rises in the daytime lasts long, but a night breeze soon falls.

12. In every army, the five developments connected with fire must be known, the movements of the stars calculated, and a watch kept for the proper days.

13. Hence those who use fire as an aid to the attack show intelligence; those who use water as an aid to the attack gain an accession of strength.

14. By means of water, an enemy may be intercepted, but not robbed of all his belongings.

15. Unhappy is the fate of one who tries to win his battles and succeed in his attacks without cultivating the spirit of enterprise; for the result is waste of time and general stagnation.

16. Hence the saying: The enlightened ruler lays his plans well ahead; the good general cultivates his resources.

17. Move not unless you see an advantage; use not your troops unless there is something to be gained; fight not unless the position is critical.

18. No ruler should put troops into the field merely to gratify his own spleen; no general should fight a battle simply out of pique.

19. If it is to your advantage, make a forward move; if not, stay where you are.

20. Anger may in time change to gladness; vexation may be succeeded by content.

21. But a kingdom that has once been destroyed can never come again into being; nor can the dead ever be brought back to life.[33]

22. Hence the enlightened ruler is heedful, and the good general full of caution. This is the way to keep a country at peace and an army intact.

---

[33] This point is at the heart of Sun Tzu's ethical philosophy and should be considered carefully by any would-be combatant. Note in chapter VI of the *Tao Te Ching*: "Weapons, however beautiful, are instruments of ill omen, hateful to all creatures. Therefore he who has Tao will have nothing to do with them." Also in chapter VIII of the *Tao Te Ching*: "The violent and stiff-necked die not by a natural death."

XIII.

The Use Of Spies

1. Sun Tzu said: Raising a host of a hundred thousand men and marching them great distances entails heavy loss on the people and a drain on the resources of the State. The daily expenditure will amount to a thousand ounces of silver. There will be commotion at home and abroad, and men will drop down exhausted on the highways. As many as seven hundred thousand families will be impeded in their labor.

2. Hostile armies may face each other for years, striving for the victory which is decided in a single day. This being so, to remain in ignorance of the enemy's condition simply because one grudges the outlay of a hundred ounces of silver in honors and emoluments, is the height of inhumanity.

3. One who acts thus is no leader of men, no present help to his sovereign, no master of victory.

4. Thus, what enables the wise sovereign and the good general to strike and conquer, and achieve things beyond the reach of ordinary men, is foreknowledge.

5. Now this foreknowledge cannot be elicited from spirits; it cannot be obtained inductively from experience, nor by any deductive calculation.

6. Knowledge of the enemy's dispositions can only be obtained from other men.

7. Hence the use of spies, of whom there are five classes:
     (1) Local spies;
     (2) inward spies;
     (3) converted spies;
     (4) doomed spies;
     (5) surviving spies.

8. When these five kinds of spy are all at work, none can discover the secret system. This is called "divine manipulation of the threads." It is the sovereign's most precious faculty.

9. Having *local spies* means employing the services of the inhabitants of a district.

10. Having *inward spies*, making use of officials of the enemy.

11. Having *converted spies*, getting hold of the enemy's spies and using them for our own purposes.

12. Having *doomed spies*, doing certain things openly for purposes of deception, and allowing our spies to know of them and report them to the enemy.

13. *Surviving spies*, finally, are those who bring back news from the enemy's camp.

14. Hence it is that which none in the whole army are more intimate relations to be maintained than with spies. None should be more liberally rewarded. In no other business should greater secrecy be preserved.

15. Spies cannot be usefully employed without a certain intuitive sagacity.

16. They cannot be properly managed without benevolence and straightforwardness.

17. Without subtle ingenuity of mind, one cannot make certain of the truth of their reports.

18. Be subtle! be subtle! and use your spies for every kind of business.

19. If a secret piece of news is divulged by a spy before the time is ripe, he must be put to death together with the man to whom the secret was told.

20. Whether the object be to crush an army, to storm a city, or to assassinate an individual, it is always necessary to begin by finding out the names of the attendants, the aides-de-camp, and door-keepers and sentries of the general in command. Our spies must be commissioned to ascertain these.

21. The enemy's spies who have come to spy on us must be sought out, tempted with bribes, led away and comfortably housed. Thus they will become converted spies and available for our service.

22. It is through the information brought by the converted spy that we are able to acquire and employ local and inward spies.

23. It is owing to his information, again, that we can cause the doomed spy to carry false tidings to the enemy.

24. Lastly, it is by his information that the surviving spy can be used on appointed occasions.

25. The end and aim of spying in all its five varieties is knowledge of the enemy; and this knowledge can only be derived, in the first instance, from the converted spy. Hence it is essential that the converted spy be treated with the utmost liberality.

26. Of old, the rise of the Yin dynasty was due to I Chih who had served under the Hsia. Likewise, the rise of the Chou dynasty was due to Lu Ya who had served under the Yin.[34]

27. Hence it is only the enlightened ruler and the wise general who will use the highest intelligence of the army for purposes of spying and thereby they achieve great results. Spies are a most important element in water, because on them depends an army's ability to move.

---

[34] Sun Tzu is observing that these dynasties arose due to shifting allegiances and changing of sides—hence, a former minister bringing vital information into another's camp.

TAO TE CHING

The Sayings of Lao Tzu

Contents

I.

Tao in its Transcendental Aspect and in its Physical Manifestation

The Tao which can be expressed in words is not the eternal Tao; the name which can be uttered is not its eternal name. Without a name, it is the Beginning of Heaven and Earth; with a name, it is the Mother of all things. Only one who is eternally free from earthly passions can apprehend its spiritual essence; he who is ever clogged by passions can see no more than its outer form. These two things, the spiritual and the material, though we call them by different names, in their origin are one and the same. This sameness is a mystery,—the mystery of mysteries. It is the gate of all spirituality.

How unfathomable is Tao! It seems to be the ancestral progenitor of all things. How pure and clear is Tao! It would seem to be everlasting. I know not of whom it is the offspring. It appears to have been anterior to any Sovereign Power.

Tao eludes the sense of sight, and is therefore called colorless. It eludes the sense of hearing, and is therefore called soundless. It eludes the sense of touch, and is therefore called incorporeal. These three qualities cannot be apprehended, and hence they may be blended into unity.

Its upper part is not bright, and its lower part is not obscure. Ceaseless in action, it cannot be named, but returns again to nothingness. We may call it the form of the formless, the image of the imageless, the fleeting and the indeterminable. Would you go before it, you cannot see its face; would you go behind it, you cannot see its back.

The mightiest manifestations of active force flow solely from Tao.

Tao in itself is vague, impalpable,—how impalpable, how vague! Yet within it there is Form. How vague, how impalpable! Yet within it there is Substance. How profound, how obscure! Yet within it there is a Vital Principle. This principle is the Quintessence of Reality, and out of it comes Truth.

From of old until now, its name has never passed away. It watches over the beginning of all things. How do I know this about the beginning of things? Through Tao.

There is something, chaotic yet complete, which existed before Heaven and Earth. Oh, how still it is, and formless, standing alone without changing, reaching everywhere without suffering harm! It must be regarded as the Mother of the Universe. Its name I know not. To designate it, I call it Tao. Endeavoring to describe it, I call it Great. Being great, it passes on; passing on, it becomes remote; having become remote, it returns.

Therefore Tao is great; Heaven is great; Earth is great; and the Sovereign also is great. In the Universe there are four powers, of which the Sovereign is one. Man takes his law from the Earth; the Earth takes its law from Heaven; Heaven takes its law from Tao; but the law of Tao is its own spontaneity.

Tao in its unchanging aspect has no name. Small though it be in its primordial simplicity, mankind dare not claim its service. Could princes and kings hold and keep it, all creation would spontaneously pay homage. Heaven and Earth would unite in sending down sweet dew, and the people would be righteous unbidden and of their own accord.

As soon as Tao creates order, it becomes nameable. When it once has a name, men will know how to rest in it. Knowing how to rest in it, they will run no risk of harm.

Tao as it exists in the world is like the great rivers and seas which receive the streams from the valleys.

All-pervading is the Great Tao. It can be at once on the right hand and on the left. All things depend on it for life, and it rejects them not. Its task accomplished, it takes no credit. It loves and nourishes all things, but does not act as master. It is ever free from desire. We may call it small. All things return to it, yet it does not act as master. We may call it great.

The whole world will flock to him who holds the mighty form of Tao. They will come and receive no hurt, but find rest, peace, and tranquility.

With music and dainties we may detain the passing guest. But if we open our mouths to speak of Tao, he finds it tasteless and insipid.

Not visible to the sight, not audible to the ear, in its use it is inexhaustible.

Retrogression is the movement of Tao. Weakness is the character of Tao.

All things under Heaven derive their being from Tao in the form of Existence; Tao in the form of Existence sprang from Tao in the form of Non-Existence.

Tao is a great square with no angles, a great vessel which takes long to complete, a great sound which cannot be heard, a great image with no form.

Tao lies hid and cannot be named, yet it has the power of transmuting and perfecting all things.

Tao produced Unity; Unity produced Duality; Duality produced Trinity; and Trinity produced all existing objects. These myriad objects leave darkness behind them and embrace the light, being harmonized by the breath of Vacancy.

Tao produces all things; its Virtue nourishes them; its Nature gives them form; its Force perfects them.

Hence there is not a single thing but pays homage to Tao and extols its Virtue. This homage paid to Tao, this extolling of its Virtue, is due to no command, but is always spontaneous.

Thus it is that Tao, engendering all things, nourishes them, develops them, and fosters them; perfects them, ripens them, tends them, and protects them.

Production without possession, action without self-assertion, development without domination this is its mysterious operation.

The World has a First Cause, which may be regarded as the Mother of the World. When one has the Mother, one can know the Child. He who knows the Child and still keeps the Mother, though his body perish, shall run no risk of harm.

It is the Way of Heaven not to strive, and yet it knows how to overcome; not to speak, and yet it knows how to obtain a response; it calls not, and things come of themselves; it is slow to move, but excellent in its designs.

Heaven's net is vast; though its meshes are wide, it lets nothing slip through.

The Way of Heaven is like the drawing of a bow: it brings down what is high and raises what is low. It is the Way of Heaven to take from those who have too much, and give to those who have too little. But the way of man is not so. He takes away from those who have too little, to add to his own superabundance. What man is there that can take of his own superabundance and give it to mankind? Only he who possesses Tao.

The Tao of Heaven has no favorites. It gives to all good men without distinction.

Things wax strong and then decay. This is the contrary of Tao. What is contrary to Tao soon perishes.

II.

Tao as a Moral Principle, or "Virtue"

The highest goodness is like water, for water is excellent in benefiting all things, and it does not strive. It occupies the lowest place, which men abhor. And therefore it is near akin to Tao.

When your work is done and fame has been achieved, then retire into the background; for this is the Way of Heaven.

Those who follow the Way desire not excess; and thus without excess they are forever exempt from change.

All things alike do their work, and then we see them subside. When they have reached their bloom, each returns to its origin. Returning to their origin means rest or fulfillment of destiny. This reversion is an eternal law. To know that law is to be enlightened. Not to know it, is misery and calamity. He who knows the eternal law is liberal-minded. Being liberal-minded, he is just. Being just, he is kingly. Being kingly, he is akin to Heaven. Being akin to Heaven, he possesses Tao. Possessed of Tao, he endures forever. Though his body perish, yet he suffers no harm.

He who acts in accordance with Tao, becomes one with Tao. He who treads the path of Virtue becomes one with Virtue. He who pursues a course of Vice becomes one with Vice. The man who is one with Tao, Tao is also glad to receive. The man who is one with Virtue, Virtue is also glad to receive. The man who is one with Vice, Vice is also glad to receive.

He who is self-approving does not shine. He who boasts has no merit. He who exalts himself does not rise high. Judged according to Tao, he is like remnants of food or a tumor on the body—an object of universal disgust. Therefore one who has Tao will not consort with such.

Perfect Virtue acquires nothing; therefore it obtains everything. Perfect Virtue does nothing, yet there is nothing which it does not effect. Perfect Charity operates without the need of anything to evoke it. Perfect Duty to one's neighbor operates, but always needs to be evoked. Perfect Ceremony operates, and calls for no outward response; nevertheless it induces respect.

Ceremonies are the outward expression of inward feelings.

If Tao perishes, then Virtue will perish; if Virtue perishes, then Charity will perish; if Charity perishes, then Duty to one's neighbor will perish; if Duty to one's neighbor perishes, then Ceremonies will perish.

Ceremonies are but the veneer of loyalty and good faith, while oft-times the source of disorder. Knowledge of externals is but a showy ornament of Tao, while oft-times the beginning of imbecility.

Therefore the truly great man takes his stand upon what is solid, and not upon what is superficial; upon what is real, and not upon what is ornamental. He rejects the latter in favor of the former.

When the superior scholar hears of Tao, he diligently practices it. When the average scholar hears of Tao, he sometimes retains it, sometimes loses it. When the inferior scholar hears of Tao, he loudly laughs at it. Were it not thus ridiculed, it would not be worthy of the name of Tao.

He who is enlightened by Tao seems wrapped in darkness. He who is advanced in Tao seems to be going back. He who walks smoothly in Tao seems to be on a rugged path.

The man of highest virtue appears lowly. He who is truly pure behaves as though he were sullied. He who has virtue in abundance behaves as though it were not enough. He who is firm in virtue seems like a skulking pretender. He who is simple and true appears unstable as water.

If Tao prevails on earth, horses will be used for purposes of agriculture. If Tao does not prevail, war-horses will be bred on the common.

If we had sufficient knowledge to walk in the Great Way, what we should most fear would be boastful display.

The Great Way is very smooth, but the people love the by-paths.

Where the palaces are very splendid, there the fields will be very waste, and the granaries very empty.

The wearing of gay embroidered robes, the carrying of sharp swords, fastidiousness in food and drink, super-abundance of property and wealth: this I call flaunting robbery; most assuredly it is not Tao.

He who trusts to his abundance of natural virtue is like an infant newly born, whom venomous reptiles will not sting, wild beasts will not seize, birds of prey will not strike. The infant's bones are weak, its sinews are soft, yet its grasp is firm. All day long it will cry without its voice becoming hoarse. This is because the harmony of its bodily system is perfect.

Temper your sharpness, disentangle your ideas, moderate your brilliancy, live in harmony with your age. This is being in conformity with the principle of Tao. Such a man is impervious alike to favor and disgrace, to benefits and injuries, to honor and contempt. And therefore he is esteemed above all mankind.

In governing men and in serving Heaven, there is nothing like moderation. For only by moderation can there be an early return to man's normal state. This early return is the same as a great storage of Virtue. With a great storage of Virtue there is naught which may not be achieved. If there is naught which may not be achieved, then no one will know to what extent this power reaches. And if no one knows to what extent a man's power reaches, that man is fit to be the ruler of a State. Having the secret of rule, his rule shall endure. Setting the tap-root deep, and making the spreading roots firm: this is the way to ensure long life to the tree.

Tao is the sanctuary where all things find refuge, the good man's priceless treasure, the guardian and savior of him who is not good.

Hence at the enthronement of an Emperor and the appointment of his three ducal ministers, though there be some who bear presents of costly jade and drive chariots with teams of four horses, that is not so good as sitting still and offering the gift of this Tao.

Why was it that the men of old esteemed this Tao so highly? Is it not because it may be daily sought and found, and can remit the sins of the guilty? Hence it is the most precious thing under Heaven.

All the world says that my Tao is great, but unlike other teaching. It is just because it is great that it appears unlike other teaching. If it had this likeness, long ago would its smallness have been known.

The skillful philosophers of the olden time were subtle, spiritual, profound, and penetrating. They were so deep as to be incomprehensible. Because they are hard to comprehend, I will endeavor to describe them.

Shrinking were they, like one fording a stream in winter. Cautious were they, like one who fears an attack from any quarter. Circumspect were they, like a stranger guest; self-effacing, like ice about to melt; simple, like unpolished wood; vacant, like a valley; opaque, like muddy water.

When terms are made after a great quarrel, a certain ill-feeling is bound to be left behind. How can this be made good? Therefore, having entered into an agreement, the Sage adheres to his obligations, but does not exact fulfillment from others. The man who has Virtue attends to the spirit of the compact; the man without Virtue attends only to his claims.

He who tries to govern a kingdom by his sagacity is of that kingdom the despoiler; but he who does not govern by sagacity is the kingdom's blessing. He who understands these two sayings may be regarded as a pattern and a model. To keep this principle constantly before one's eyes is called Profound Virtue. Profound Virtue is unfathomable, far-reaching, paradoxical at first, but afterwards exhibiting thorough conformity with Nature.

III.

The Doctrine of Inaction

The Sage occupies himself with inaction, and conveys instruction without words. Is it not by neglecting self-interest that one will be able to achieve it?

Purge yourself of your profound intelligence, and you can still be free from blemish. Cherish the people and order the kingdom, and you can still do without meddlesome action.

Who is there that can make muddy water clear? But if allowed to remain still, it will gradually become clear of itself. Who is there that can secure a state of absolute repose? But let time go on, and the state of repose will gradually arise.

Be sparing of speech, and things will come right of themselves.

A violent wind does not outlast the morning; a squall of rain does not outlast the day. Such is the course of Nature. And if Nature herself cannot sustain her efforts long, how much less can man!

Attain complete vacuity, and sedulously preserve a state of repose.

Tao is eternally inactive, and yet it leaves nothing undone. If kings and princes could but hold fast to this principle, all things would work out their own reformation. If, having reformed, they still desired to act, I would have them restrained by the simplicity of the Nameless Tao. The simplicity of the Nameless Tao brings about an absence of desire. The absence of desire gives tranquility. And thus the Empire will rectify itself.

The softest things in the world override the hardest. That which has no substance enters where there is no crevice. Hence I know the advantage of inaction.

Conveying lessons without words, reaping profit without action,—there are few in the world who can attain to this!

Activity conquers cold, but stillness conquers heat. Purity and stillness are the correct principles for mankind.

Without going out of doors one may know the whole world; without looking out of the window, one may see the Way of Heaven. The further one travels, the less one may know. Thus it is that without moving you shall know; without looking you shall see; without doing you shall achieve.

The pursuit of book-learning brings about daily increase. The practice of Tao brings about daily loss.

Repeat this loss again and again, and you arrive at inaction. Practice inaction, and there is nothing which cannot be done.

The Empire has ever been won by letting things take their course. He who must always be doing is unfit to obtain the Empire.

Keep the mouth shut, close the gateways of sense, and as long as you live you will have no trouble. Open your lips and push your affairs, and you will not be safe to the end of your days.

Practice inaction, occupy yourself with doing nothing.

Desire not to desire, and you will not value things difficult to obtain. Learn not to learn, and you will revert to a condition which mankind in general has lost.

Leave all things to take their natural course, and do not interfere.

IV.

Lowness and Humility

All things in Nature work silently. They come into being and possess nothing. They fulfill their functions and make no claim.

When merit has been achieved, do not take it to yourself; for if you do not take it to yourself, it shall never be taken from you.

Follow diligently the Way in your own heart, but make no display of it to the world.

Keep behind, and you shall be put in front; keep out, and you shall be kept in.

Goodness strives not, and therefore it is not rebuked.

He that humbles himself shall be preserved entire. He that bends shall be made straight. He that is empty shall be filled. He that is worn out shall be renewed. He who has little shall succeed. He who has much shall go astray.

Therefore the Sage embraces Unity, and is a model for all under Heaven. He is free from self-display, therefore he shines forth; from self-assertion, therefore he is distinguished; from self-glorification, therefore he has merit; from self-exaltation, therefore he rises superior to all. Inasmuch as he does not strive, there is no one in the world who can strive with him.

He who, conscious of being strong, is content to be weak, he shall be the paragon of mankind. Being the paragon of mankind, Virtue will never desert him. He returns to the state of a little child.

He who, conscious of his own light, is content to be obscure,—he shall be the whole world's model. Being the whole world's model, his Virtue will never fail. He reverts to the Absolute.

He who, conscious of desert, is content to suffer disgrace,—he shall be the cynosure of mankind. Being the cynosure of mankind, his Virtue then is full. He returns to perfect simplicity.

He who is great must make humility his base. He who is high must make lowliness his foundation. Thus, princes and kings in speaking of themselves use the terms "lonely," "friendless," "of small account." Is not this making humility their base?

Thus it is that "Some things are increased by being diminished, others are diminished by being increased." What others have taught, I also teach; verily, I will make it the root of my teaching.

What makes a kingdom great is its being like a down-flowing river,—the central point towards which all the smaller streams under Heaven converge; or like the female throughout the world, who by quiescence always overcomes the male. And quiescence is a form of humility.

Therefore, if a great kingdom humbles itself before a small kingdom, it shall make that small kingdom its prize. And if a small kingdom humbles itself before a great kingdom, it shall win over that great kingdom. Thus the one humbles itself in order to attain, the other attains because it is humble. If the great kingdom has no further desire than to bring men together and to nourish them, the small kingdom will have no further desire than to enter the service of the other. But in order that both may have their desire, the great one must learn humility.

The reason why rivers and seas are able to be lords over a hundred mountain streams, is that they know how to keep below them. That is why they are able to reign over all the mountain streams.

Therefore the Sage, wishing to be above the people, must by his words put himself below them; wishing to be before the people, he must put himself behind them. In this way, though he has his place above them, the people do not feel his weight; though he has his place before them, they do not feel it as an injury. Therefore all mankind delight to exalt him, and weary of him not.

The Sage expects no recognition for what he does; he achieves merit but does not take it to himself; he does not wish to display his worth.

I have three precious things, which I hold fast and prize. The first is gentleness; the second is frugality; the third is humility, which keeps me from putting myself before others. Be gentle, and you can be bold; be frugal, and you can be liberal; avoid putting yourself before others, and you can become a leader among men.

But in the present day men cast off gentleness, and are all for being bold; they spurn frugality, and retain only extravagance; they discard humility, and aim only at being first. Therefore they shall surely perish.

Gentleness brings victory to him who attacks, and safety to him who defends. Those whom Heaven would save, it fences round with gentleness.

The best soldiers are not warlike; the best fighters do not lose their temper. The greatest conquerors are those who overcome their enemies without strife. The greatest directors of men are those who yield place to others. This is called the Virtue of not striving, the capacity for directing mankind; this is being the compeer of Heaven. It was the highest goal of the ancients.

V.

Government

Not exalting worth keeps the people from rivalry. Not prizing what is hard to procure keeps the people from theft. Not to show them what they may covet is the way to keep their minds from disorder.

Therefore the Sage, when he governs, empties their minds and fills their bellies, weakens their inclinations and strengthens their bones. His constant object is to keep the people without knowledge and without desire, or to prevent those who have knowledge from daring to act. He practices inaction, and nothing remains ungoverned.

He who respects the State as his own person is fit to govern it. He who loves the State as his own body is fit to be entrusted with it.

In the highest antiquity, the people did not know that they had rulers. In the next age they loved and praised them. In the next, they feared them. In the next, they despised them.

How cautious is the Sage, how sparing of his words! When his task is accomplished and affairs are prosperous, the people all say: "We have come to be as we are, naturally and of ourselves."

If anyone desires to take the Empire in hand and govern it, I see that he will not succeed. The Empire is a divine utensil which may not be roughly handled. He who meddles, mars. He who holds it by force, loses it.

Fishes must not be taken from the water: the methods of government must not be exhibited to the people.

Use uprightness in ruling a State; employ stratagems in waging war; practice non-interference in order to win the Empire. Now this is how I know what I lay down:—

As restrictions and prohibitions are multiplied in the Empire, the people grow poorer and poorer. When the people are subjected to overmuch government, the land is thrown into confusion. When the people are skilled in many cunning arts, strange are the objects of luxury that appear.

The greater the number of laws and enactments, the more thieves and robbers there will be. Therefore the Sage says: "So long as I do nothing, the people will work out their own reformation. So long as I love calm, the people will right themselves. If only I keep from meddling, the people will grow rich. If only I am free from desire, the people will come naturally back to simplicity."

If the government is sluggish and tolerant, the people will be honest and free from guile. If the government is prying and meddling, there will be constant infraction of the law. Is the government corrupt? Then uprightness becomes rare, and goodness becomes strange. Verily, mankind have been under delusion for many a day!

Govern a great nation as you would cook a small fish.

If the Empire is governed according to Tao, disembodied spirits will not manifest supernatural powers. It is not that they lack supernatural power, but they will not use it to hurt mankind. Again, it is not that they are unable to hurt mankind, but they see that the Sage also does not hurt mankind. If then neither Sage nor spirits work harm, their virtue converges to one beneficent end.

In ancient times those who knew how to practice Tao did not use it to enlighten the people, but rather to keep them ignorant. The difficulty of governing the people arises from their having too much knowledge.

If the people do not fear the majesty of government, a reign of terror will ensue.

Do not confine them within too narrow bounds; do not make their lives too weary. For if you do not weary them of life, then they will not grow weary of you.

If the people do not fear death, what good is there in using death as a deterrent? But if the people are brought up in fear of death, and we can take and execute any man who has committed a monstrous crime, who will dare to follow his example?

Now, there is always one who presides over the infliction of death. He who would take the place of the magistrate and himself inflict death, is like one who should try to do the work of a master-carpenter. And of those who try the work of a master-carpenter there are few who do not cut their own hands.

The people starve because those in authority over them devour too many taxes; that is why they starve. The people are difficult to govern because those placed over them are meddlesome; that is why they are difficult to govern. The people despise death because of their excessive labor in seeking the means of life; that is why they despise death.

A Sage has said: "He who can take upon himself the nation's shame is fit to be lord of the land. He who can take upon himself the nation's calamities is fit to be ruler over the Empire."

Were I ruler of a little State with a small population, and only ten or a hundred men available as soldiers, I would not use them. I would have the people look on death as a grievous thing, and they should not travel to distant countries. Though they might possess boats and carriages, they should have no occasion to ride in them. Though they might own weapons and armor, they should have no need to use them. I would make the people return to the use of knotted cords. They should find their plain food sweet, their rough garments fine. They should be content with their homes, and happy in their simple ways. If a neighboring State was within sight of mine—nay, if we were close enough to hear the crowing of each other's cocks and the barking of each other's dogs—the two peoples should grow old and die without there ever having been any mutual intercourse.

VI.

War

He who serves a ruler of men in harmony with Tao will not subdue the Empire by force of arms. Such a course is wont to bring retribution in its train.

Where troops have been quartered, brambles and thorns spring up. In the track of great armies there must follow lean years.

The good man wins a victory and then stops; he will not go on to acts of violence. Winning, he boasteth not; he will not triumph; he shows no arrogance. He wins because he cannot choose; after his victory he will not be overbearing.

Weapons, however beautiful, are instruments of ill omen, hateful to all creatures. Therefore he who has Tao will have nothing to do with them.

Where the princely man abides, the weak left hand is in honor. But he who uses weapons honors the stronger right. Weapons are instruments of ill omen; they are not the instruments of the princely man, who uses them only when he needs must. Peace and tranquility are what he prizes. When he conquers, he is not elate. To be elate were to rejoice in the slaughter of human beings. And he who rejoices in the slaughter of human beings is not fit to work his will in the Empire.

On happy occasions, the left is favored; on sad occasions, the right. The second in command has his place on the left, the general in chief on the right. That is to say, they are placed in the order observed at funeral rites. And, indeed, he who has exterminated a great multitude of men should bewail them with tears and lamentation. It is well that those who are victorious in battle should be placed in the order of funeral rites.

A certain military commander used to say: "I dare not act the host; I prefer to play the guest. I dare not advance an inch; I prefer to retreat a foot."

There is no greater calamity than lightly engaging in war. Lightly to engage in war is to risk the loss of our treasure.

When opposing warriors join in battle, he who has pity conquers.

VII.

Paradoxes

Among mankind, the recognition of beauty as such implies the idea of ugliness, and the recognition of good implies the idea of evil. There is the same mutual relation between existence and non-existence in the matter of creation; between difficulty and ease in the matter of accomplishing; between long and short in the matter of form; between high and low in the matter of elevation; between treble and bass in the matter of musical pitch; between before and after in the matter of priority.

Nature is not benevolent; with ruthless indifference she makes all things serve their purposes, like the straw dogs we use at sacrifices. The Sage is not benevolent: he utilizes the people with the like inexorability.

The space between Heaven and Earth,—is it not like a bellows? It is empty, yet inexhaustible; when it is put in motion, more and more comes out.

Heaven and Earth are long-lasting. The reason why Heaven and Earth can last long is that they live not for themselves, and thus they are able to endure.

Thirty spokes unite in one nave; the utility of the cart depends on the hollow centre in which the axle turns. Clay is moulded into a vessel; the utility of the vessel depends on its hollow interior. Doors and windows are cut out in order to make a house; the utility of the house depends on the empty spaces.

Thus, while the existence of things may be good, it is the non-existent in them which makes them serviceable.

When the Great Tao falls into disuse, benevolence and righteousness come into vogue. When shrewdness and sagacity appear, great hypocrisy prevails. It is when the bonds of kinship are out of joint that filial piety and paternal affection begin. It is when the State is in a ferment of revolution that loyal patriots arise.

Cast off your holiness, rid yourself of sagacity, and the people will benefit an hundredfold. Discard benevolence and abolish righteousness, and the people will return to filial piety and paternal love. Renounce your scheming and abandon gain, and thieves and robbers will disappear. These three precepts mean that outward show is insufficient, and therefore they bid us be true to our proper nature;—to show simplicity, to embrace plain dealing, to reduce selfishness, to moderate desire.

A variety of colors makes man's eye blind; a diversity of sounds makes man's ear deaf; a mixture of flavors makes man's palate dull.

He who knows others is clever, but he who knows himself is enlightened. He who overcomes others is strong, but he who overcomes himself is mightier still. He is rich who knows when he has enough. He who acts with energy has strength of purpose. He who moves not from his proper place is long-lasting. He who dies, but perishes not, enjoys true longevity.

If you would contract, you must first expand. If you would weaken, you must first strengthen. If you would overthrow, you must first raise up. If you would take, you must first give. This is called the dawn of intelligence.

He who is most perfect seems to be lacking; yet his resources are never outworn. He who is most full seems vacant; yet his uses are inexhaustible.

Extreme straightness is as bad as crookedness. Extreme cleverness is as bad as folly. Extreme fluency is as bad as stammering.

Those who know do not speak; those who speak do not know.

Abandon learning, and you will be free from trouble and distress.

Failure is the foundation of success, and the means by which it is achieved. Success is the lurking-place of failure; but who can tell when the turning-point will come?

He who acts, destroys; he who grasps, loses. Therefore the Sage does not act, and so does not destroy; he does not grasp, and so he does not lose.

Only he who does nothing for his life's sake can truly be said to value his life.

Man at his birth is tender and weak; at his death he is rigid and strong. Plants and trees when they come forth are tender and crisp; when dead, they are dry and tough. Thus rigidity and strength are the concomitants of death; softness and weakness are the concomitants of life.

Hence the warrior that is strong does not conquer; the tree that is strong is cut down. Therefore the strong and the big take the lower place; the soft and the weak take the higher place.

There is nothing in the world more soft and weak than water, yet for attacking things that are hard and strong there is nothing that surpasses it, nothing that can take its place.

The soft overcomes the hard; the weak overcomes the strong. There is no one in the world but knows this truth, and no one who can put it into practice.

Those who are wise have no wide range of learning; those who range most widely are not wise.

The Sage does not care to hoard. The more he uses for the benefit of others, the more he possesses himself. The more he gives to his fellow-men, the more he has of his own.

The truest sayings are paradoxical.

VIII.

Miscellaneous Sayings and Precepts

By many words wit is exhausted; it is better to preserve a mean. The excellence of a dwelling is its site; the excellence of a mind is its profundity; the excellence of giving is charitableness; the excellence of speech is truthfulness; the excellence of government is order; the excellence of action is ability; the excellence of movement is timeliness.

He who grasps more than he can hold, would be better without any. If a house is crammed with treasures of gold and jade, it will be impossible to guard them all.

He who prides himself upon wealth and honor hastens his own downfall. He who strikes with a sharp point will not himself be safe for long.

He who embraces unity of soul by subordinating animal instincts to reason will be able to escape dissolution. He who strives his utmost after tenderness can become even as a little child.

If a man is clear-headed and intelligent, can he be without knowledge?

The Sage attends to the inner and not to the outer; he puts away the objective and holds to the subjective.

Between yes and yea, how small the difference!

Between good and evil, how great the difference!

What the world reverences may not be treated with disrespect.

He who has not faith in others shall find no faith in them.

To see oneself is to be clear of sight. Mighty is he who conquers himself.

He who raises himself on tiptoe cannot stand firm; he who stretches his legs wide apart cannot walk.

Racing and hunting excite man's heart to madness.

The struggle for rare possessions drives a man to actions injurious to himself.

The heavy is the foundation of the light; repose is the ruler of unrest.

The wise prince in his daily course never departs from gravity and repose. Though he possess a gorgeous palace, he will dwell therein with calm indifference. How should the lord of a myriad chariots conduct himself with levity in the Empire? Levity loses men's hearts; unrest loses the throne.

The skillful traveler leaves no tracks; the skillful speaker makes no blunders; the skillful reckoner uses no tallies. He who knows how to shut uses no bolts—yet you cannot open. He who knows how to bind uses no cords—yet you cannot undo.

Among men, reject none; among things, reject nothing. This is called comprehensive intelligence.

The good man is the bad man's teacher; the bad man is the material upon which the good man works. If the one does not value his teacher, if the other does not love his material, then despite their sagacity they must go far astray. This is a mystery of great import.

As unwrought material is divided up and made into serviceable vessels, so the Sage turns his simplicity to account, and thereby becomes the ruler of rulers.

The course of things is such that what was in front is now behind; what was hot is now cold; what was strong is now weak; what was complete is now in ruin. Therefore the Sage avoids excess, extravagance, and grandeur.

Which is nearer to you, fame or life? Which is more to you, life or wealth? Which is the greater malady, gain or loss?

Excessive ambitions necessarily entail great sacrifice. Much hoarding must be followed by heavy loss. He who knows when he has enough will not be put to shame.

He who knows when to stop will not come to harm. Such a man can look forward to long life.

There is no sin greater than ambition; no calamity greater than discontent; no vice more sickening than covetousness. He who is content always has enough.

Do not wish to be rare like jade, or common like stone.

The Sage has no hard and fast ideas, but he shares the ideas of the people and makes them his own. Living in the world, he is apprehensive lest his heart be sullied by contact with the world. The people all fix their eyes and ears upon him. The Sage looks upon all as his children.

I have heard that he who possesses the secret of life, when traveling abroad, will not flee from rhinoceros or tiger; when entering a hostile camp, he will not equip himself with sword or buckler. The rhinoceros finds in him no place to insert its horn; the tiger has nowhere to fasten its claw; the soldier has nowhere to thrust his blade. And why? Because he has no spot where death can enter.

To see small beginnings is clearness of sight. To rest in weakness is strength.

He who knows how to plant, shall not have his plant uprooted; he who knows how to hold a thing, shall not have it taken away. Sons and grandsons will worship at his shrine, which shall endure from generation to generation.

Knowledge in harmony is called constant. Constant knowledge is called wisdom. Increase of life is called felicity. The mind directing the body is called strength.

Be square without being angular. Be honest without being mean. Be upright without being punctilious. Be brilliant without being showy.

Good words shall gain you honor in the marketplace, but good deeds shall gain you friends among men.

To the good I would be good; to the not-good I would also be good, in order to make them good.

With the faithful I would keep faith; with the unfaithful I would also keep faith, in order that they may become faithful.

Even if a man is bad, how can it be right to cast him off?

Requite injury with kindness.

The difficult things of this world must once have been easy; the great things of this world must once have been small. Set about difficult things while they are still easy; do great things while they are still small. The Sage never affects to do anything great, and therefore he is able to achieve his great results.

He who always thinks things easy is sure to find them difficult. Therefore the Sage ever anticipates difficulties, and thus it is he never encounters them.

While times are quiet, it is easy to take action; ere coming troubles have cast their shadows, it is easy to lay plans.

That which is brittle is easily broken; that which is minute is easily dissipated. Take precautions before the evil appears; regulate things before disorder has begun.

The tree which needs two arms to span its girth sprang from the tiniest shoot. Yon tower, nine storeys high, rose from a little mound of earth. A journey of a thousand miles began with a single step.

A great principle cannot be divided; therefore it is that many containers cannot contain it.

The Sage knows what is in him, but makes no display; he respects himself, but seeks not honor for himself.

To know, but to be as though not knowing, is the height of wisdom. Not to know, and yet to affect knowledge, is a vice. If we regard this vice as such, we shall escape it. The Sage has not this vice. It is because he regards it as a vice that he escapes it.

Use the light that is in you to revert to your natural clearness of sight. Then the loss of the body is unattended by calamity. This is called doubly enduring.

In the management of affairs, people constantly break down just when they are nearing a successful issue. If they took as much care at the end as at the beginning, they would not fail in their enterprises.

He who lightly promises is sure to keep but little faith.

He whose boldness leads him to venture, will be slain; he who is brave enough not to venture, will live. Of these two, one has the benefit, the other has the hurt. But who is it that knows the real cause of Heaven's hatred? This is why the Sage hesitates and finds it difficult to act.

The violent and stiff-necked die not by a natural death.

True words are not fine; fine words are not true.

The good are not contentious; the contentious are not good.

This is the Way of Heaven, which benefits, and injures not. This is the Way of the Sage, in whose actions there is no element of strife.

IX.

Lao Tzu on Himself

Alas! the barrenness of the age has not yet reached its limit. All men are radiant with happiness, as if enjoying a great feast, as if mounted on a tower in spring. I alone am still, and give as yet no sign of joy. I am like an infant which has not yet smiled, forlorn as one who has nowhere to lay his head. Other men have plenty, while I alone seem to have lost all. I am a man foolish in heart, dull and confused. Other men are full of light; I alone seem to be in darkness. Other men are alert; I alone am listless. I am unsettled as the ocean, drifting as though I had no stopping-place. All men have their usefulness; I alone am stupid and clownish. Lonely though I am and unlike other men, yet I revere the Foster-Mother, Tao.

My words are very easy to understand, very easy to put into practice; yet the world can neither understand nor practice them.

My words have a clue, my actions have an underlying principle. It is because men do not know the clue that they understand me not.

Those who know me are but few, and on that account my honor is the greater.

Thus the Sage wears coarse garments, but carries a jewel in his bosom.

Integrated Index

This integrated index is designed to cross reference concepts in both The Art of War *(designated as AW) and the* Tao Te Ching *(designated as TTC).*

life
    secret of, 146 (TTC)
    softness/weakness and, 142, 143 (TTC)
    war as matter of death and, 23 (AW)
    See also death
living off the land, 31, 32, 88 (AW)
local spies, 102, 104 (TTC)
loyalty, 119, 140 (TTC)
lures/bait, 26, 48, 51, 64, 66–67, 71–73, 78, 104 (AW)

M

maneuvering, 59–64 (AW)
    deviation in, 59, 62, 91 (AW)
    difficulty of, 59 (AW)
    direct and indirect methods in, 45–47 (AW)
    familiarity with terrain, 61, 82–83, 94 (AW)
    flexibility in, 45–47 (AW)
    night-maneuvers, 60, 62 (AW)

risks of alliances, 61 (AW)
risks of marches, 60 (AW)
See also marching
mantlets/screens, 36, 72 (AW)
marching, 69–75 (AW)
    avoiding dangerous country, 71 (AW)
    encampment. *See* encampment
    familiarity with terrain, 61, 82–83, 94 (AW)
    in flat country, 70 (AW)
    mountain warfare, 64, 69, 71, 78–79 (AW)
    risks of marches, 60 (AW)
    river warfare, 69–70, 71 (AW)
    salt-marsh warfare, 70 (AW)
    signs of enemy advance and retreat, 72–74 (AW)
    See also maneuvering

About the Authors

Little is known about **Sun Tzu**, who is estimated to have been born in 544 BC in the latter-era of China's Zhou dynasty, and died in 496 BC. According to posthumous records, Sun Tzu—an honorific title meaning "Master Sun"—was a commander in the dynastic army. His ancient treatise on strategy is one of the most widely read works of antiquity.

Lionel Giles, whose groundbreaking 1905 translation of the *Tao Te Ching* and 1910 translation of *The Art of War* appear in this volume, was a British sinologist and curator at the British Museum. Giles also translated the works of Confucius, Mencius, and several classical landmarks of Chinese philosophy. Born in 1875, he died in 1958.

Lightning Source UK Ltd.
Milton Keynes UK
UKHW021436260721
387791UK00017B/393

9 781722 505608